dream
CATCHER

An ENTREPRENEUR'S
Journey from DREAM *to Success*

Jennifer Jansch

Art direction by Annaminh Braun
Photos by Jennifer Jansch,
Linda Alfvegren, Jenny Brandt

You can be the dream
CATCHER

Sometimes in life you just have to go ahead and JUMP straight into the unknown in order to follow your DREAMS. That's what I did, and it paid off in a big way!

Jennifer in the Bag-all store
on Mott Street in NYC.

Five years ago, my husband and I sold our home and all our furniture in Stockholm and said bye-bye to everything we had in terms of security in order to follow our dream of living in New York City. Many people thought this was incredibly irresponsible, especially since we have three daughters to provide for. Honestly, I agreed with them. In Sweden we both had great jobs, but in New York we had nothing. No contacts, no clients, no safety net. But I did have something: a dream.

"*Feel the* FEAR . . . *and do it* ANYWAY!"

—Susan Jeffers

My dream was this: to start my own business. Now, there was a slight problem with my dream; I had no idea what my business should be. I knew it had to be something environmentally friendly, and other than that my head was blank. It was a very bizarre situation where I knew I needed to look for something, but I didn't know *what* I was looking for. Imagine searching for a needle in a haystack without knowing it is the needle you're looking for. Even if you were to find it, you wouldn't know that was *it*. I felt very overwhelmed, lost, and full of fear of our uncertain future.

In that negative state of mind, I started looking for things that could take me out of this dark place and help keep me on my quest. I felt that reading about the stories of people who had made similar journeys was very helpful. There were always bits and pieces I could apply to my own life. I started collecting inspirational quotes. Whenever fear would take an ice cold-grip on me, I would look at these quotes and lead my mind to a more positive place.

I felt that regular "start your own business" books were not for me. They were technical, uninspiring, and, most important, based on the premise that you already had an idea. Which I didn't.

With this book, I would like to give the advice, tips, and *inspiration* I wished I had during this period. I truly believe that each and every one of us can and should follow our dreams in order to live a happy and fulfilling life.

Unfortunately there are many people out there who will give you all the reasons for why you can't follow your dream—or you might be telling yourself those same things. There are also plenty of people who think that things can only be done in one way. Well, I disagree. There are as many ways of following your dreams as there are people. A business can be started on a shoestring, just like mine was. Bag-all was built bag by bag, without financing. It can be done without any kind of business training and knowledge about production or selling products. It can even be done without an idea. But you do need to have one thing: *a dream.*

This is my journey—making my dream come true. Hopefully it will inspire you to follow your own path.

When you decide to do something new in life, it often comes after a long period of thinking about change. I had a very successful career as a stylist in Sweden. I had worked in the fashion industry since I was sixteen years old and got my first job as a stylist for a teen magazine. I definitely had an interest in fashion all my life, but I always had a hard time taking it seriously. Honestly, clothes are not that important, but the people in the industry talk about fashion as if there really is some vital importance to the world whether pants are baggy or tight this season. So, although I was doing very well and supporting myself and my family for many years as a stylist, it did not give me a sense of purpose.

Becoming a mother also changed me. I started thinking about the environment in a more long-term perspective. This planet needs to last for our children and their children's children . . . My concern grew to a sense of urgency. I wanted to stop thinking about it and start *doing* something to improve it.

In addition to not feeling a sense of purpose, I wanted to be more in charge of my time — not having to be somewhere eight hours a day and having the freedom to live anywhere on the planet. I understood that in order to be "free" I needed to make more money.

I worked very hard for many years, creating value for other people. For instance, a friend and I had started a glossy magazine, *Mama*, for mothers in Sweden. She came up with the idea for the magazine and I packaged it as a glamorous oasis for moms drowning in diapers and baby food. *Mama* really took off and became a huge success. However, it was owned by a large publishing house, and I was only seeing my salary and none of the profits.

I knew people who were writers and singers, and I saw that they were selling their creations over and over again. Getting the benefits of royalties and reprints. Yet as a stylist, I would only get paid once for each job, no matter how much energy and creativity I poured into it or how many times my pictures were published. So I concluded that I needed to create some kind of product in order to capitalize on my creativity. Something that could be sold more than once.

"You don't have to be great to START, but you have to start to be GREAT."

—Zig Ziglar

Here is what I knew at that point:

1. In order to be happy I needed to do something that filled me with a sense of purpose.
2. In order for it to have a sense of purpose, it had to be something environmentally friendly.
3. In order to be "free," I needed to earn more money and create value for myself rather than for others.
4. To capitalize on my creativity, I needed to create something that could be sold over and over again.

These realizations got me started on my next step: *list-making*.

My three girls, Celeste, Margaux, and Caprice, hugging it out in Big Sur, California. Becoming a mother made me increasingly worried about the future of our planet.

Starting the ... LIST MAKING

It is really hard to make a list when you don't know what your end goal is. But I had a blue notebook where I would write down scattered ideas. Sometimes it would be just one word. I knew that writing things down would not only help me remember my ideas but also start the process of thoughts transforming into actions and objects.

1 The first thing I wrote on my list was:
- **ECO-FRIENDLY**

I wanted to do something that felt important on a deeper level. Something that would not only pay the bills but also actually benefit the environment in the long run.

"WRITING things down starts the process of THOUGHTS transforming into actions and OBJECTS."

2 Then, some weeks later I wrote:
- **WORK FROM HOME**

I knew that we didn't have very much money to start whatever idea I might come up with. So my business needed to be something I could run out of my own home.

It's up to you to make it Happen!

3
- **CHEAP**

The product must be cheap to develop. Again, we didn't have much money, so the initial investment could not be that big. Developing a product can cost thousands of dollars, and we just didn't have that kind of money.

4 **• GEOGRAPHICALLY INDEPENDENT**
I wanted to be able to work from anywhere in the world.
Thinking about being geographically independent led me to point 5.

5 **• WEB-BASED**
I understood that it needed
to be a product that could
be sold on the Internet in
order for me to be able to
work from anywhere.

6 **• FLAT AND LIGHT**
My product needed to be
flat and light in order to be
shipped, as you need to do
when you have a webshop.
Also, I understood that I
would need to house the
product in our home, and
therefore it couldn't be
very big.

And so my list continued. And
continued . . .

I believe that the list not only
helped me remember all of my
ideas, but it also made me able to
RECOGNIZE the IDEA when
I finally came across it.

She turned

into cans

into

During the list-making process, I kept coming up with different ideas for what my business could be. One idea was to make small fabric bags for jewelry. I searched the net to see what was out there. I came across some smaller businesses selling reusable fabric gift bags. I loved this idea!

However, I was not loving the design of the bags as much. As a stylist, a big part of my life has been about style and form. I would have loved to use gift bags at home, but there was no way I would have *those* patterns under my Christmas tree. This may seem superficial, but design is very important to me and I think we all deserve to be surrounded by nice objects.

I believe the best way to get people to change their habits is through good design. Tesla is a great example, where the car is so good-looking you would get it even if it wasn't the best choice for the environment. What I loved most about the bags was the fact that they are reusable. I had discovered these bags right after Christmas, and that year I had truly been bothered by the amount of garbage our family of five had accumulated. Black garbage bag after garbage bag . . . In New York, trash is put out on the curb, so I could see that every single house had just as much trash as we did.

Then something struck me: *MY LIST!*

The bags were flat, easy to store, easy to ship, had a good price range, and, most important, were reusable. The list had made it possible for me to recognize my idea when I finally came across it. I had found that needle in the haystack. It had taken five years . . .

I was going to make beautifully designed **reusable gift bags!**

Beautiful Stockholm at dusk on a winter day.

*her can'ts
and dreams
plans.*

SOME FACTS ABOUT REUSE

There are so many wonderful things about reuse, but most importantly reusing is something anybody can do, and I mean anybody. It doesn't matter if you are rich or poor (in fact, poor people are—much better at reusing than more privileged groups), young or old, or where you live in the world. It is so, so easy—you just take an item and use it again. Each time you reuse something, it replaces a product that would otherwise have been produced. For instance, if you buy a bottle of water and fill it up again when it's empty, it replaces the new plastic bottle you otherwise would have bought. Which brings me to another fantastic thing about reuse: it's free!

Let me give you an example of what reusing just **one** plastic bottle, by simply filling an old bottle with tap water, saves the environment from:

• **the garbage the bottle would have become**, had you not reused it.

• **the usage of natural resources** needed to make a new bottle.

• **the energy produced** in order to make the new bottle.

• **the toxic waste** from the process of making a new plastic bottle.

• **the transportation** (often across the oceans) needed to ship the new bottle to your location.

• **the energy spent** on keeping the new bottle cooled.

• and finally the **transportation to the waste plant.**

I totally understand that we do need some packaging for food, although I am convinced we could find a system to refill packages in the stores, like milk bottles in the old days.

How to get that VINTAGE STYLE

Reuse is GENIUS in so many ways. It saves you money, anyone can do it, and, on top of that, it's the most STYLISH thing.

Our old apartment in Stockholm. Almost everything was from flea markets and cheap auction houses.

The philosophy of Bag-all is based on the idea of reuse. At a very young age I started living a "reuse lifestyle" even though I was not aware of it myself. I was interested in fashion and would always be on the lookout for unique things to wear. I didn't have very much money and realized that I would get more bang for my buck if I bought vintage clothes. I would, of course, also raid my mother's closet for clothes I could somehow change into fashion pieces.

When I eventually got my first home, I started looking for vintage furniture. It was what I could afford, but mostly I was fascinated by the look of older items.

Later in life I continued to buy older furniture. In our Stockholm home, almost every item was vintage. Not the expensive, antique kind of vintage, but pieces from flea markets and cheap auction houses. This look intrigued people so much that our home was featured in many magazines and books across the world.

There are a lot of things that we don't need to buy over and over. Almost everything we own can be reused and repurposed. Reuse does not need to be boring or unstylish. Quite the opposite. Take a look at how to make a dress from a T-shirt on page 121.

Another fantastic advantage of reuse, particularly when it comes to furniture, is that what you paid for something is most likely what someone else will pay when you are ready to part with it. If you purchase something at an auction, you are very likely to get the most fair price. If someone is bidding against you, the price goes up; if not, the price goes down. The items are worth exactly what someone is willing to pay for them.

Generally, old furniture is also of better quality and will last much longer.

"Unless someone like YOU cares a whole awful lot, nothing is going to get better. It's NOT."

—Dr. Seuss

If you are fortunate enough to inherit furniture, the pieces also have a history that means something to you, as opposed to buying something new. Think about it. The minute you bring a new sofa out of the store, it loses half of its value. If you use it for five to ten years it will probably be in such bad shape you would have to pay someone to come take it away. And, of course, it becomes a huge piece of garbage that needs to be disposed of.

Having our whole house full of vintage pieces meant that when we decided to move to New York and sold all our furniture, we got the money we had spent on it back and then some. It turned out we had this furniture "for free" all those years.

Find more about reuse, gift bags, and how to make them yourself on page 38.

Everything in this picture is vintage except the table, which I had made from a round piece of plywood and mounted on legs from IKEA. The chairs are classical Swedish chairs called "Göteborgsstolen" (the "Gothenburg chair") and were bought for under $30 each. That's what I call a bargain considering the amazing design and craftmanship.

Welcome to the jungle room. the carpet in our bedroom was a leftover piece from the sixties.

On the bed rests our eighteen-year-old Abyssinian, Ping.

Celeste's room with bed and armchair bought in a web auction.

KITCHEN CHAIRS
Bamboo imitation chairs found on eBay. I then had them spray painted by a company that spray paints kitchen cabinets.

COLLECTING STUFF
I have always liked to collect things, like white porcelain. The items are very undervalued so you can make bargains.

CHESTERFIELD SOFA
Old Chesterfield sofas are very undervalued and can be purchased cheaply. I love the look of an old tufted leather sofa.

PHOTO SHOOT

This picture is from a photo shoot I did a few years back with my youngest daughter, Caprice, and my oldest, Celeste. Caprice is wearing a vintage romper bought at a flea market.

vintage
WONDERS

FLOWER POWER

Margaux, to the left, in a beautiful hand-sewn dress that cost $5.

This dress was made for my mother by my grandmother. Now it is Margaux's turn.

FOLKLORE

Caprice in a vintage Swedish folklore dress.

Vintage clothes are great, in particular those for children. Children grow so fast they rarely wear out nicer pieces such as dresses. This means that there are lots of old children's garments available for very little money.

MORE REASONS
to wear vintage clothes:

1 **EACH PIECE** is unique.

2 **IT HAS A POSITIVE** environmental impact.

3 **GREAT QUALITY**
   Many old pieces of clothes are hand sewn.

4 **GOOD INVESTMENT**
   Cheap to buy, and clothes can be resold.

P. S. Remember to pass on your children's and your own clothes to others.

17

Celeste jumping in a field in Skåne, south part of Sweden.

moving to the city OF DREAMS

In 2011 we finally moved to NEW YORK CITY. We knew that if we didn't move now, it would never HAPPEN.

Manhattan view from Top of the Rock at Rockefeller Center.

Photo: Linda Alfvegren

*"The secret of getting AHEAD is getting started.
The secret of getting started is breaking your
complex overwhelming tasks into small
MANAGEABLE tasks, and starting on the first one."*

—Mark Twain

The first few months in New York were very tough. We didn't have any source of income, and it was clear that in order for us to accomplish our dream of living in New York permanently we needed to get some sort of business off the ground.

I had been working on my list of ideas for years, and I knew I loved the idea of reusable gift bags. That was about all I knew, because I truly had no idea how to make these bags into a reality. Much less how to sell them to other people.

However, I am incredibly optimistic, always thinking things are going to be easy and fast. When I first got the idea, I thought: *Fabric bags—how hard can it be? This is going to be eeeaaasssyy breeezzzyy.* Of course, little did I know that it would take me over a year to figure out how to construct them, print the fabrics, and have them produced. I have zero patience and hate to wait. (Honestly, I kind of feel that the Universe had sent me the Bag-all project as a test of my character. *How much waiting can she take before she goes completely insane?*)

Although I was optimistic, there was something that really bothered me about my idea: Other people didn't believe in the bags. Generally, when I do something in life I ask people what they think of my idea. I find that getting their input is valuable, as I can always learn something and tweak my ideas. Normally, some people like an idea and some people don't. But this time everyone had more or less negative opinions.

I saw a couple of major drawbacks with the idea myself.

1. SIMILAR BUSINESSES HAD FAILED

There were a very small number of people on the web who understood the idea of reusable gift bags. Why had this idea not caught on?

One could easily tell that the webshops selling the gift bags were not established, flourishing brands. In fact most of the websites I saw at that time are now gone. So this was clearly a risky business.

2. PEOPLE DIDN'T "GET" IT

A gift bag is a tough sell. Let's say you want to launch a T-shirt brand. You know for sure that people use T-shirts, so there is a fair chance they will buy your shirts. In this case I knew for sure that I didn't know anyone who had ever purchased a reusable gift bag. Also, a gift bag requires an explanation. Just looking at it won't automatically tell you what it is and why you need to buy it.

On top of this, I had zero business training. I didn't know the first thing about writing a business plan (other than my long list); I couldn't read a balance sheet; we had little money to invest; and I didn't know anything about production, sales, wholesale, retail or building a website. You name it, I didn't know how to do it. The odds were clearly stacked up against me. Did I let that stop me? No! Was I scared? You bet!

But guess what—the same was true for having my first child. I didn't know anything about babies, but that didn't stop me and my husband. I am guessing most of those people who think they can't start their own business or follow their dreams still have children, even though they didn't know much about babies in advance. You simply learn as you go along. In my opinion, having children and raising them requires the same effort as starting your own business. Bag-all has most definitely become my fourth child.

Here they are ...
6 good THINGS

to consider if you are feeling LOST and don't know how to get STARTED on your dream.

What isn't tried won't work.

—Claude McDonald

1 GET UNSTUCK

In the beginning, I had no clue how to do any of the things I needed to do to create Bag-all. I was complaining to a friend about how stuck I was, and I didn't know how to continue with my idea. He had only two words for me: *Get unstuck!*

Somehow that made me pick myself up and continue. Two steps ahead, one step back . . . two steps ahead, three steps back . . . uphill. But, as in exercising, the more you practice walking uphill, the stronger you get.

2 DO IT SCARED

If you feel scared, keep going and follow your dreams anyway. Obviously you shouldn't jump off a cliff, but quite often it's the new and unknown that scares us most. And very often these new challenges are "keys" that show us the way forward. Doing the "same old" is easy and safe, but it leads us nowhere (unless that "same old" is what you are passionate about and love doing).

It's all about your state of mind: One of my favorite quotes of all time is by Henry Ford (the farmer boy who founded Ford Motors): "*Whether you think you can or whether you think you can't—you're right.*" Meaning if you tell yourself that you *can* do something, you are much more likely to succeed than if you tell yourself you *can't*.

"The way to get started is to quit TALKING and start DOING."

—Walt Disney

3 START BEFORE YOU'RE READY

Don't sit around and wait for the right time to get started. If you do, you'll come up with tons of reasons for not getting started. The habit of "starting before you are ready" is a common trait among successful people. Be brave—stop procrastinating and take the first step, even if it seems outlandish.

Celeste with Bag-all's
World Traveller
shopping totev.

4 CHERISH PROBLEMS —
BECAUSE THEY WILL COME!

In the beginning I constantly came across problems—and I still do. When my first shipment of bags arrived, the prints did not come out right and they were so poorly sewn I couldn't sell most of them . . . This was, of course, a disaster as I didn't have a backup. But I had to focus my attention on which bags I *could sell* and put the problem bags at the back of my mind.

Problems can really get you down, unless you understand that the secret to your success is to EXPECT problems. Don't presume everything will go exactly as you planned. Be in a mindset of: *Problems are guidelines, not stop signs.* They are there to teach us things about our business and life in general. Once you start expecting problems, they stop affecting you in a really negative way and they don't zap your energy. Problems will always be annoying, of course, as they slow you down. But more often than not problems will lead you to a better route.

Remember: Changing your original plan is not failure, it's being smart and adaptable! If you don't change your path when you come across a problem, it will appear again and again, and each time on a larger scale. We can only move on in life when we learn from our mistakes—and we can only learn from our mistakes if we acknowledge them and *own* them. Every time a problem arises in my life, no matter how *unfair* it seems, I ask myself: *What was my part in this?* Once I see my own part, I can truly learn and avoid the same thing in the future.

23

5

PRAISE YOURSELF AND CELEBRATE SMALL VICTORIES

An important thing to do when you start a business, and really any time in life, is to focus on the things you DO accomplish. Don't focus too much on what you didn't get done. Put those things on a to-do list (don't think you can keep it all in your head; you need to have it on a list) and then put your attention on all the things you have gotten done, big and small, during the day. I bet you will realize that it is a lot.

Besides, it is great to celebrate small victories. Perhaps you finally got a nice sample that you're happy with. Take the time to celebrate it. Buy yourself a drink or flowers. It just makes life more fun!

Once you realize how accomplished you are, you will start feeling proud. Allow yourself to give yourself praise: "*Wow, I did a really good job today.*" The feeling of pride automatically leads to a feeling of gratitude. Which brings me to point 6 . . .

"More people would LEARN *from their mistakes if they weren't so busy* DENYING *them."*

—Harold J. Smith

P.S. Read more about Praise and Gratitude on page 99–101

6

BE GRATEFUL

There are so many fantastic quotes about gratitude. Here are two of my favorites:

"The first step to being great is being grateful."
—Anonymous

"Saying thank you is not only good manners. It's good spirituality."
—Alfred Painter

The more gratitude you feel toward what you have in your life, big and small stuff, the more goodness you will attract. I find this as true for business as for anything else.

It seems to me that the world in general works pretty much in the same way as people do. Let's say someone gives you a gift or does you a favor; if you show this person how grateful you are, the person is more likely to do it again.

Saying *thank you* costs absolutely nothing and takes no effort, so why not say it? In our family, we practice gratitude by saying three or more things we are grateful for at the dinner table. I think it is especially good for kids to do this since human beings have a tendency to take things for granted.

I truly believe anyone can start their own business or pursue their dreams (not everyone wants to be an entrepreneur). Don't let thoughts of all the things you don't know how to do limit you. Rest assured you will learn how to do them along the way. And on the ride, enjoy each problem and count your blessings.

everything
is ok
in the end
if it's not
then
it's not
the end

This is a painting
I did a few years
back. I love
the message,
attributed to John
Lennon.

Yesterday is
history.
tomorrow
is a
mystery.
today is
a gift —
that is why
it is called
the present.

—Anonymous

This is the table we set up for Margaux's tenth birthday. Gift bags and strawberry cake.

THE creation
OF A PRODUCT

I finally had my IDEA and was ready to start bringing it to LIFE. But how?

PLEASE *reuse*

waste REDUCE

At this point I had my idea—the reusable gift bag. Now, how was I going to take them from idea to reality? I tried doing research about how to sew a gift bag. There was no good information online and no books I could find. I realized I would have to make them myself and use the ancient method of "trial and error."

I did have a sewing machine, but I didn't know how to sew very well. So I started to experiment with all sorts of different constructions of the bags. Lined bags, bags with a drawstring on top and in the middle, bags without a bottom, and bags with a bottom.

> *"I haven't FAILED.*
> *I have just found 10,000 ways*
> *that won't WORK."*
>
> —Thomas Edison

In the end I decided on a bag with a bottom very similar to a paper bag so it can be folded flat. This way the bag would stand when something was put inside. Also, the bag has a grosgrain ribbon about two inches from the top so it can be easily closed. This bag is what we still sell today. On page 38, you can learn how to make them yourself.

Once I had the construction of the bag down, I started looking for eco-friendly fabrics for my bags. I figured that I would buy prints I liked and have

This is one of the first bags I made. A seamstress in a small village close to our summerhouse showed me how to sew a lined bag. This one is lined with a natural linen fabric.

the bags made in those fabrics. However, I quickly started to see that eco-friendly fabrics are very expensive and that if I used them, the price point of the bags would skyrocket. Another problem was that the available prints were not in the colors and patterns I envisioned for my first collection. I wanted the prints to match in color and scale so all bags could be used together.

Many hours spent at the sewing machine in our summerhouse.

Unfortunately, I was unsuccessful in finding a producer in New York who could make the bags at a price that would be reasonable to build a business on. I realized that the bags would have to compete with the price of wrapping paper. Customers would look at Bag-all bags and calculate whether they would go for a gift bag or continue using paper.

I definitely did not want the bags to be a luxury item only a few select people could afford. I figured that I would rather make the bags available to many people than do everything "right" in terms of using local production and materials.

I started looking at having the bags produced in Asia as that would give me a lower price point. However, the transportation of my bags is still concerning to me, and I am looking into having them made in the US for the US market.

On a positive note: Bag-all has grown very rapidly in Asia. For the customers in that region, Bag-all's bags are truly locally produced.

As I wanted everything to be as environmentally friendly as possible, I planned to have the bags produced locally in the Garment District of New York. To find a producer, I wandered the streets in the Garment District, knocking on hundreds of doors. I remember feeling so lost and hopeless. How was I going to get this thing off the ground?

Here the gift bags are printed with eco-friendly colors.

KRYSSA PATTERN

I used a white-out pen to create the Kryssa pattern. Left is my hand drawn sample, and above are how the bags came out.

VISITING FACTORIES

As Bag-all has grown, I try to visit factories and suppliers in China and other countries as well. It gives me a better understanding of their situation and they understand me better as well

POORLY SEWN BAGS

Most of the bags in my first order were unsellable. This is an example of what the bags looked like.

F inding good producers is hard and very time consuming. I found factories in China by searching online. I put together an email, introducing myself and my business idea to thirty factories.

Some of the factories didn't answer at all and others answered but didn't speak English very well. Since I don't speak Chinese, I had to eliminate them. So I continued the email conversation with only five of the original thirty factories.

Most Chinese factories have very high minimum orders, but they understand that they need to help new businesses as well. It is very important to let them know your situation and how far along your company has come.

Next, ask for samples: this is a crucial step. You can tell by the time it takes to get the sample and, of course, the quality of the sample, whether the factory is good or not. You always have to pay for samples, but some factories charge way more than others. I weed them out straight away as I don't want to work with people who are not fair.

It's a very time-consuming process, but trust me— doing a thorough job in the beginning pays off. Once I was communicating directly with the factories, I quickly understood that I wasn't going to find prints that I liked in China. Remember, Bag-all was started because I didn't like the patterns I saw on existing fabric gift bags. Then the factories informed me that they could do screen prints of any design I liked. This opened up new possibilities, but all of a sudden I would have to become a pattern designer as well.

This was such a fun thing! I began working really hard on putting together a collection of prints in stripes, checks and dots in complementary colors that would go nicely together. I hand drew the patterns since I didn't know how to draw on a computer. I chose the colors very carefully to match each other. Then, I held my breath and placed my first order. The factory said they wouldn't do less than four thousand pieces—this was a staggering number to me. What was I going to do with four thousand bags if no one wanted to buy them?

I waited and waited. When the bags finally arrived we excitedly tore open the boxes—the colors did not match each other at all. And what was worse, they were so poorly sewn I knew I could not sell most of them.

Margaux with one of the first gift bags.

5 Genius
THINGS ABOUT REUSABLE BAGS

1 YOU NEVER HAVE TO BUY . . .

. . .wrapping paper, string, and tape again.

2 VERY CHEAP. After many uses, your bag can be considered almost free.

3 WRAPPING your gifts will take no more than ten seconds. Just pop your gift in the bag and you are good to go!

4 NO GARBAGE—zero.

5 DON'T HAVE TO GIVE THEM AWAY. Many people don't think about the fact that you don't have to give the bags away, you can just keep them in the family. This is what we do. We have about twenty bags that we give back and forth to each other. In a family of five that is many times a year: five birthdays a year, Christmas, Father's and Mother's day, Easter, etc . . . We store them flat in a drawer, just like bed linen, between uses, and that way they are ready to go next time we need them.

The price of GIFT WRAPPING

STAGGERING NUMBERS

- In order to make paper, nearly **4 billion** trees around the globe are harvested yearly.

- Unfortunately, the paper-making process is not a clean one. According to the US Toxic Release Inventory report published by the EPA, pulp and paper mills are among the **worst polluters to air, water, and land** of any industry.

- Most popular wrapping paper is dyed and laminated and contains non-paper additives such as gold- and silver-colored shapes or glitter, which **cannot be recycled**. This means paper is either dumped in the trash or, worse, put in the recycling bin, which will mean the **whole lot** is contaminated and has to go to **landfill**.

- According to the *Wall Street Journal*, gift wrapping sales in the US totaled **$9.36 billion** in 2010 (more than the combined GDP of Africa's **nine poorest** countries).

The more I learn about **reusing**, the more I understand that **reusing** is clearly the best way to do something for our planet. The most effective way to reduce waste is to *not create it in the first place*. Making a new product requires raw materials that must be extracted from the earth, and the product must be fabricated and transported to wherever it will be sold. And then disposed. By reduction and reuse, we can save natural resources, protect the environment, and save money.

> I typically don't like to print things on paper, but spreading the message of reuse is so important it needs to be communicated in every way possible.

* Numbers from: www.epa.gov

STATISTICS ON GIFT WRAPPING

- **Americans throw away 25 percent** more trash during the holiday season. The extra waste amounts to **25 million tons** of garbage. Approximately 4 million of those tons are from gift wrapping.*

- So great is the **British passion** for cards and the wrapping of gifts with elaborate ribbons and bows that each Christmas they collectively throw away 226,800 miles of wrapping paper, which is enough to stretch nine times around the world, according to *The Telegraph*.

- If every American would **reuse** just 24 inches of holiday ribbon, it would be enough to **tie a bow around the Earth!***

- If every US family wrapped just three presents in **reused material**, that would save paper equivalent to **45,000 football fields.***

ABOUT realistic CHANGE

Bag-all is based on ideas of sustainability and reuse. In my opinion, we need to go toward change through INSPIRING, rather then scaring, people to change their habits. I don't believe in a fear-based way of living. Good design is a great way to inspire people to make better choices. If a product is attractive and functional, people will buy it, use it, and hopefully *reuse* it.

I also believe we have to be practical and realistic about environmental issues. For instance, Bag-all's bags are not made of organic cotton. The simple reason is that organic cotton is still too expensive and would put a price tag on the bags that no one would like to pay. So, I had to decide whether I wanted to try to introduce reusable gift bags on a large scale or not at all. I decided that it was better to go ahead with my idea although I knew I wouldn't be able to do everything completely green to begin with. I figured if I could get the message out about reuse, that would be more important. Also, I felt that if this business was successful, I could eventually have the products made in the most environmentally friendly way as possible. Meanwhile, we try to do everything else as environmentally friendly as we can at Bag-all (see page 110).

My daugthers at the end of a pier in Gotland, an island in the south of Sweden.

get the party started
REUSE

I LOVE the concept of REUSE and gift bags so much I want to share how you can make them YOURSELF.

3&4

1

2

5

7

6

8

9

To make your own gift bag, you can use any fabric. It could be an old tea towel, a curtain, or piece of clothing. Reusing materials is fun and makes the bag more interesting and attractive.

Making the bag takes no more then twenty minutes. Remember, there are many ways to make a bag and there are no rules. This shows you how to make the bags Bag-all sells; there is also a video on how to make them on www.bag-all.com.

Good luck! And do send us photos of yours!

This is. HOW you do it:

1 **CUT YOUR FABRIC** into a rectangle shape. We are making a small bag so we used the measurement 20x15 inches.

2 **LOCATE WHERE YOUR BUTTON** hole is going. This is where your string is going to come out, so it needs to be located in the center 4 to 6 inches from the top. If you have a program on your sewing machine to stitch button holes, use it to create the opening for the string.

3 **ZIGZAG ALL SIDES** of the fabric. This makes the bag more sturdy and prevents fraying of the fabric.

4 **FOLD THE FABRIC** in half along the button hole. Your bag is inside out at this point. Sew a straight seam along the side that is going to be the back of the bag.

5 **TO CREATE THE BOTTOM** of the bag, fold in the sides 2 inches on each side. The bag is still inside out. Sew a straight line across the bottom.

6 **TURN THE BAG THE RIGHT WAY** and fold the bottom flat like a paper bag.

7 **TO CREATE A TUNNEL** for your string, fold the top of the bag and iron it flat.

8 **STITCH ON EACH SIDE** of the button hole.

9 **THREAD THE RIBBON** through the tunnel. You can use a safety pin or a paper clip to do it.

10 Voilà! Your bag is done. Enjoy!

KID STUFF
Using fabric bags is a great way to organize your children's toys.

making
bags
of
DREAMS

There are no RULES when creating something. Think outside the BOX.

JEWELRY

Small bags can store your jewelry; plus they look super cute on your vanity table.

BAG INSPIRATION

Before I started Bag-all, I spent a whole summer sewing different kinds of bags to see which models and what kinds of patterns worked best.

Now that you know how to make the bags yourself, let your imagination take you away and create the bags of your dreams . . .

This is the first bag I ever made. It was a rectangle-shaped bag with no bottom and a silk ribbon tied around it.

Margaux holding a bag with a skull pattern and yellow and white dots on the interior.

41

I do love a good quote. Like this one: *"The best things in life are free."* The same goes for reusing (and quotes).

Another thing that is free is advice. People are incredibly generous in giving their opinion if you ask them. I always ask others what they think about a new print, how things can be done in a better way, what the best item is on the menu, etc.

I also love to give advice!

However, I've noticed that many people get offended when they are given advice. They seem to believe that the advice holds some hidden criticism. This is truly a shame, as so many of the best things I have done in life have been influenced by advice I've received from others.

My initial idea for Bag-all was to only sell reusable fabric gift bags. I had no other thought in my mind. But as per usual, I was asking every person I talked to what they thought about the idea. I had made several bags myself and given them to friends and family. To my surprise, people were rather negative. Not that they didn't like the bag they had received, but most thought the bags could never be a real business. At the same time, they would tell me how they were using the bags for other things than gifts. One friend told me she put her hair dryer in it because she always had problems finding a place for it. My mom used her bag to carry high heels when going to parties (in Sweden everybody brings a pair of "inside shoes" when they are invited to friends' houses). I started to notice a pattern . . .

People obviously needed bags for many things besides presents. This new insight immediately went to the top of my list!

THE good ADVICE
you should SOMETIMES *listen to and the opinions you can* IGNORE.

Pompes

Chaussures

Maquillage

Bijoux

Celeste with the French
Collection at our summer-
house in Sweden.

I have to admit that I was rather discouraged by what people had to say about my new business idea. No one believed in it. Everyone gave me many reasons for why I should not go ahead.

Which brings me to another important thing about advice—*you don't have to take it.* Let your heart tell you which is good advice and which is not.

People often want to warn you out of concern,

Good advice is free. Not because it is worthless, but because it is priceless.

—Anonymous

because they don't want to see you fail.

This fear-based way of thinking won't work if you want to create something new. You simply will have to take chances.

In my case, I decided that in the end the idea of reuse was more important to spread than choosing a safer path. I followed my gift bag dream—despite all the warnings.

But, by listening to other people, I realized that I needed to *add* something to Bag-all. People clearly needed bags for storage, organization, and travel, so I decided to develop an "Organizing Collection" in addition to the gift bags.

The Organizing/Travel Collection turned out to be a massive hit! The gift bags are coming along a bit more slowly. The way I see it is that the organizing collection is sponsoring the gift bags, until people fully understand the idea and importance of reuse.

Without the Organizing Collection, Bag-all would not have been around today. There is no way the income from the gift bag sales would have been enough to sustain a business. So thanks to listening to people's advice, Bag-all is thriving. And more importantly, thanks to ignoring some advice, it exists!

SKETCHING ON BAGS

As per usual, I didn't know how to do the artwork for the Organizing bag on a computer, so I used the old school way—a marker. I drew the prints I wanted on the bags I had made in a linen fabric. This gave me a really good sense of where to place the patterns and how large the prints should be. We still sell the same prints today.

Hair dryer bag, before and after.

Lingerie bag

45

Downtown view from
Manhattan bridge.

START before YOU'RE READY

I needed my BUSINESS *to get off the ground* QUICKLY. *I signed up for a* GIFT SHOW *before I had one piece of product . . .*

With my husband, setting up the booth.

Most of the summer was spent on the floor painting the walls for the booth.

Bag-all LAUNCH

In the spring of 2013, I was finally at a stage where I had my idea, I had built a website (see page 52), I had made samples, and I had placed an order with a factory in China. I was ready to launch Bag-all. But how? A successful friend told me that she had launched her brand by exhibiting at a gift show in New York. So I decided to try the same thing.

Renting a ten-by-ten-foot booth was incredibly expensive: $5,500 for the four days the show lasted. If I wanted walls for the booth that would be $2,500 more. This was a huge investment and risk. Not only was it a lot of money, but my bags had not arrived from the factory yet and as usual I had NO clue how to do any of this.

The gift show was at the end of summer, so I spent the whole summer worrying about it. I was on an very tight budget and couldn't afford the $2,500 for booth walls, so I came up with an idea to paint walls on a canvas, the same kind that are used for scenery during a play. I spent a large part of that summer on the living room floor painting the walls.

My first shipment of bags showed up right before the show. Of course, most of them were so poorly sewn they could not be sold, but the booth was already paid for, so I had to carry on. Actually, if the bags had arrived earlier, I would not have had the courage to do the show. In hindsight, I am glad I started before I was ready, since the show turned out to be the perfect start for Bag-all.

On the first day of the show, I was so nervous I hardly knew what to do with myself. I told myself that even if no one placed a single order, it would still be a good thing to be at the show to get exposure. Much to my amazement, we actually wrote a couple of orders the first day. We were trying to act cool while taking the orders, but really we just wanted to scream, "YEEAAYYY!"

The gift show did help provide exposure for Bag-all some major websites discovered us there. Getting into these shows, particularly getting into the right section of a show, can be very challenging for a start-up. Here are a few important things to think about when it comes to getting the most out of a trade show:

Trade SHOWS

1 VISIT THE SHOW FIRST

If at all possible, visit the show you are interested in before deciding if you want to be part of it. Look for the section where you think your items belong.

2 PLACEMENT

My experience has been that the shows will put you in the worst spot possible when you are new. They will even put you in a completely wrong section. Do everything you can to get a good placement in the right section.

3 YOUR BOOTH

You have just seconds to get a buyer's attention. Make your booth memorable and unusual—study the competition so you stand out.

4 INFORMATION

Make a good-looking postcard with info about your brand that buyers can take with them. Many purchases happen after the show. See Bag-all's info card on page 55.

5 WEB CATALOG

Many buyers will want a line sheet (a PDF with all your items listed). We have an online catalog for buyers to view. This way we don't have to print catalogs that are both bad for the environment and expensive.

bag-all

HOME   SHOP   ABOUT ⌄   NEWS   BO

This is what
www.bag-all.com
looks like.

YOUR window TO THE WORLD

Create an AWESOME WEBSITE *for your business.*

If you are thinking about starting a business, any business, you really must have a good website. I created a website for Bag-all before I did anything else. I realized that any person or factory I contacted would first look at my site before deciding if they wanted to do business with me. I also needed a webshop so people could buy my bags directly.

Webshops are excellent because they give people all over the world access to your products 24/7 without you having to be there. You can be sitting on a beach when someone places an order. You can be sleeping in your bed and making money at the same time. The cost of running a webshop is very low compared to any other way of selling products.

I did a lot of research on which sales platform to use for Bag-all. I checked out webshops that I liked and looked for the type of platform used, which is usually listed at the bottom of the site. There are many webshop platform providers out there, so browse around to see which ones offer the best themes, deals, and support. Making sure they offer good support is vital as you will probably have to contact them from time to time.

Setting up the website was not easy and very time consuming. However, I did it myself—and if I can do it, anyone can. The tools for designing web pages are getting better all the time.

There is one very important thing to think about when starting a webshop: IT TAKES TIME for it to get going. Customers will not find your store right away. Generally, it takes a couple of years before you start making money on a webshop. But when it finally works, it is the best feeling in the world.

I remember the bliss when I got my first order! My shop had been open for a couple of weeks and it had no sales, only a handful of visitors. Needless to say, I was feeling kind of low. Then suddenly we heard a "pling" on my phone from an order coming in. My whole family jumped up and down, cheering. I remember packing the bags as nicely as I could in an envelope and getting on my bike to ride to our closest mailbox, which is about two miles away (we were at our summerhouse in Sweden). It started raining on the way there. But what did I care?! I had my first order going out.

So, though webshops take time, GO for it. Just be realistic and don't give up!

COMING UP WITH A NAME FOR YOUR BUSINESS

• Try to find a name that gives people an idea of what your business is. This eliminates several steps in communication.
• Your name **has to be** available as a domain name on the web. My first thought was Bagall, as one word. But, that name was already taken. Bag-all.com wasn't, so that's the name I chose.
• Does your name look good as a logo? While thinking of names, sketch logos.
• It can also be good to Google the name you are thinking of to make sure it is not associated with something else. Or if it means something bad in a different language.
• Do your own market survey by asking people around you what they think of the name.
• Register the name in your country. This way, you will also get to know if the name is taken.

Bag-all
GIVING IS EASY

| HOME | CATALOG ∨ | DISPLAY | VIDEOS | ABOUT US | CONTACT | SHIPPING |

Welcome to the world of Bag-all

Please reuse
Waste reduce

Having great product images is the most important part of selling online.

Wash me!

Please

Web CREATION

Creating a website is hard—and fun! Here are a few things to think about when creating a website.

1 LOOK AT SITES YOU LIKE
Analyze what is good about them. What can you apply to your website? Make a sketch of your site on paper to get a clearer idea of what you want for your store.

2 MAKE IT EASY TO NAVIGATE
The SHOP icon should be the easiest thing to find.

3 CONTACT INFO
People will want get in touch with you to ask questions. This is also a great way for buyers to find you.

4 ABOUT PAGE
Personally, I like sites where there is an ABOUT page. I like to know who I am buying my products from and why they are selling it.

5 SHIPPING & RETURNS
Your customers want to know how much shipping costs are and what your return policy is. At Bag-all, you can return anything you buy and you don't even have to tell us why.

6 GREAT PHOTOS
This is the most important piece of the puzzle. Remember, your website is the face of your company and your webshop is like a store window. Learn how to take photos yourself (page 56).

No 1
THE bag-all EDIT

The window of Plaza styles flagship store in Ginza Tokyo.

The floor tiles from Bag-all's store on Mott Street, recreated in Tokyo

1 BIG in Japan

• For one month the Japanese department store *Plaza Style* has created Bag-all pop up stores in seven of their biggest locations. *Jennifer Jansch*, the owner and founder of Bag-all, went to Tokyo for the opening of these amazing Pop-ups. All stores had different displays, yet they all had the spirit of the Bag-all store on Mott Street in NYC.

2 NEW styles

• The new prints: **Vanity set**, **Perfume** bottle and **Chunkey Necklace** were especially made for the Japanese department stores. We loved them so much so we made them for our store as well.

• **Pompoms** is another new item we love. Brightens up any bag and any day! $5 for a set of 4 poms.

Vanity set $10

Necklace $10

Perfume bottle $10

These are posts by our customer on Instagram with the #bagall

3 BEST of INSTA

• Follow Bag-all on Instagram: @bag_all to keep yourself updated on our new items. This is where we post all our new items as they come in.

There are many more products coming in the next few week, so keep an eye open!

Example of a promotional email from Bag-all.

MARKETING & NEWS LETTERS

Marketing is a complex subject. There is no one right way to do it. Here is what I found is true for Bag-all:

We have put very little money toward marketing. The online marketing we have tried has not been successful. We paid for ads on Facebook, which gave nothing in terms of sales. We did get some "likes," but we felt the likes were not from Bag-all fans but rather people clicking out of habit.

The same thing happened when we paid for ads on search sites. It didn't result in any sales. My belief is that if you have a good product it, will spread virally by itself. People will somehow find you and spread the word about your product because they love it. They will also like you more because they feel they have discovered your brand rather than having the brand forced on them through advertising. It seems to me that if people find your business by themselves, they become more genuinely engaged followers.

Two marketing tools have worked really well for Bag-all: Instagram and MailChimp. Both are free. Read more about Instagram on page 64. MailChimp is a very good site to compile your mailing list. I am sure there are many similar sites out there, but this is the one we use.

You can create newsletters with online templates. We only send newsletters when we truly have something to say, which is four to five times a year. It really pays not to waste people's time by sending them emails with no real news or offer. Our list has a 43.7 percent opening rate compared to 12.39 percent, which is the industry average. We also have very few unsubscribers, which is a good measure of effectiveness.

INFO CARD

Generally I don't like to print marketing materials as I find it environmentally wasteful, but for our first show I made a large-sized postcard (see example to the right) with information about Bag-all. My mission was to get people to understand the importance of reuse, and the gift bags require some explanation, so I felt this was the best option. We use the same cards today in all our shipments, and we hand them out in our store and at shows so people can understand what Bag-all is all about. The cards are, of course, printed on recycled paper.

BLOG

When launching Bag-all, I had a blog in Sweden on a friend's website. Luckily she is very famous in Sweden, so a lot of people saw my blog. The blog was a big help in explaining my thoughts on reuse and showing how the bags can be used.

However, as I don't want to waste people's time with nonsense, I put the bar very high for myself. Not only did I want the pictures to be awesome, but I also wanted every post to have some sort of message—a new thought or inspiration.

It was a wonderful way to connect with people, and I especially loved to read their comments. However, the blog was constantly on my mind: what would I write about next? I started to obsess over photographing every moment of the day. In the end, it added a huge level of stress to my life and I felt it was time to stop.

Today, we have a blog at www.bag-all.com where we post new styles and other things going on with Bag-all.

Bag-all
www.bag-all.com

GIFT BAGS
Bag-all makes cool and affordable fabric gift bags. Unlike wrapping paper, the bags can be used - and reused.

TRAVEL/STORAGE COLLECTION
Bag-all also presents a line of stylish travel/organizing bags with prints of all things you might want to pack or store.

PHILOSOPHY
Bag-all is a company that believes we all can make a big difference to the environment by doing small things. One of those things is starting to think "reuse".

"Reusing" has been recognized by the US Environmental Protection Agency as the most effective way of reducing waste and saving natural resources. And as an added bonus, reusing saves you money. In the US alone, 4 million tons of wrapping becomes waste each holiday season. Let's start changing this - one reusable bag at a time!

For additional info and contact please visit our website: www.bag-all.com or follow us on Instagram: @bag_all

Every little step to reducing garbage is a good one. Think: Reuse, Waste Reduce!

Jennifer Jansch, owner and founder of Bag-all.

"Life is like riding a bicycle. To keep your BALANCE you must keep MOVING."

—Albert Einstein

My husband, Micke, helping to set up the photo studio in our house.

TAKE
great
PHOTOS
You'll need them
to sell ANYTHING online . . .

To successfully launch a business online you need two kinds of pictures: product images and mood images.

When I started Bag-all, I didn't know how to photograph product images. I had been a stylist and had done tons of mood images. But a professional photographer always shot them.

I didn't have a budget to pay for a photographer, so I had to figure out how to photograph the bags myself. This was a long and tedious process. We invested in some basic lighting. I had a decent camera, and my husband and I started by trial and error.

In the beginning, we didn't even know what to put in the bags to make them look good. We eventually figured out that cereal boxes and soap boxes were good sizes. We then had to learn how to mask the images. This is a way to remove the background from the picture. There are excellent websites that let you do that online. Google "mask images" and you will find them.

It took us a year to figure out how to take really great product shots.

1 INVEST IN GOOD LIGHTING

Go to a camera store where professional photographers get their equiptment. Ask the staff what lamps you need to get an even light when shooting a product.

2 YOU DO NOT NEED . . .

. . . a professional camera. You can photograph your products with your smartphone. These days, we photograph all Bag-all products with a smartphone.

3 IF YOU ARE GOING TO MASK

Good product images normally need to be masked in order for large websites to use them. Photograph the product against a background in a contrasting color. If the background and the product are the same color, it is much harder for the computer to find where the background ends and the product begins.

Big Sur Dip Dye Tote is masked and ready to go online.

Micke holding the handles with a string.

2 reasons FOR GREAT IMAGES

1

If you have great product images, magazines and bloggers will want to use them. Bloggers and editors often take the images off our website and use them for their features. Bag-all was chosen as number three on *Harper's Bazaar*'s List of Holiday Gifts for the Stylish Jet Setter. We had no idea they were going to feature us. In fact, we had no idea they even knew Bag-all existed. Then, one day we started noticing people coming to our site from harpersbaazar.com. That's how we found out about the list. They had simply taken our photos and published them on their site, linking to us. Had we not had good product images I am quite confident it would never have happened.

I know some companies who pay bloggers to write about their products. Bag-all has never done that as we want everything that is written about the brand to be genuine. If somebody writes about Bag-all, it is because they truly like our products and not because they are paid to do so.

≡ BAZAAR   Fashion   Beauty   Celebrity   Culture   harper

Nov 12, 2015 @ 9:02 AM   The Culture List   Culture   Travel & Food   The List   Holiday 2015

#THELIST: GIFTS FOR THE STYLISH JET SETTER

Holiday wish-list essentials for every travel lover.

Pack It Up

Bag-all organizing travel bags, $10-$15, **bag-all.com**.

pop-up dollhouse book, $62. (shopbelle.com).

...60. ...m)

...PE IT UP Margo ...anese red ...th tape for ...rapping, ...maigocute .com)

TRAVEL ...en spaceship, $120. (saksfifthavenue .com)

ECO-WRAP Bag-All re-usable holiday bags, starting at $6. (bag-all .com)

We also got really lucky when we were featured in *Vanity Fair* during our first year in business. This happened because a very cool-looking older lady stopped by our booth at our first gift show. She told us she was an event planner for *Vanity Fair* and that she really liked the Bag-all idea. Soon after the show, we were contacted by an editor at the magazine and told that they had chosen Bag-all as one of their gift guide tips. The feature did not do much in terms of sales, but it has been a wonderful thing for PR. We still use these images from time to time.

Hey—Nicole Kidman on the cover, Bag-all inside!

"It is NEVER crowded along the EXTRA mile."

—Wayne Dyer

2 If you sell your products wholesale, the stores and webshops that sell your items will want to use your images 99 times out of 100. As you want all your products to do well, it is really important to supply them with great photos.

My pregnant friend Anna, Celeste, and Margaux with balloons in the middle of Amsterdam Avenue.

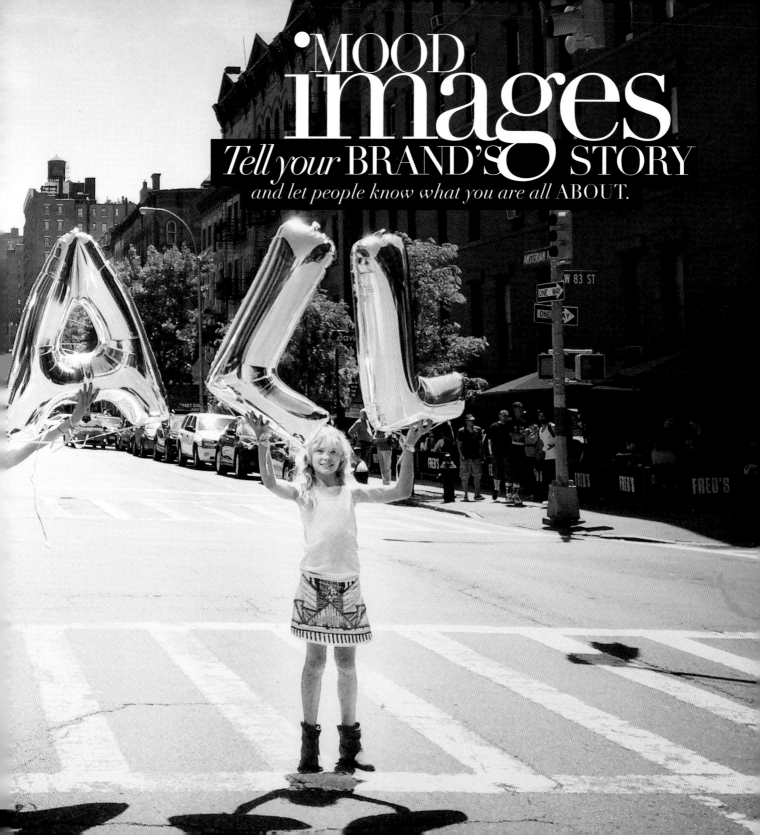

MOOD images

Tell your BRAND'S STORY

and let people know what you are all ABOUT.

My work as a stylist for over twenty years has given me insight into the old saying, *"A picture is worth a thousand words."* It's true. In less than a second, people will get a feel for your brand from an image rather than if you had to explain it to them in text. This makes mood images a very powerful tool.

Taking a good mood image requires a good idea and some planning. Of course, I have a huge advantage being a stylist (this was the one thing I did know how to do well when I started Bag-all) when it comes to photo shoots. Here are some tips on getting those memorable mood images:

A GREAT IDEA

You need an idea for your photo. To get inspiration, look at images on the Internet. All the great images since the beginning of photography are available for free for anyone to view. You can collect images in a folder and then view them as a group. You will notice a pattern of things you like and images that speak to you. Take all the great properties from these pictures and try to come up with your own idea.

I shot the image to the right after looking at pictures of New York City rooftops. I loved that some of them had balloons, and I created my own version of a girl on a rooftop with balloons.

GET GREAT PROPS

I happen to love balloons. I think they look great in photographs and add an element of fun and playfulness. I don't want Bag-all to be perceived as a snobbish high-fashion brand. I want people to feel the fun, the joy, and the accessibility of the brand. I want the message to be: "At Bag-all we don't take ourselves too seriously. There is a sense of fairy-tale and wonder. And we jump for joy!" I don't know if you get that feeling from looking at this picture, but that was my intention.

TAKE YOUR TIME

Don't expect to get it right the first time, or the second . . . As with everything else, it takes practice to take good photos. A trick of the fashion trade is to take many, many pictures. When I took the picture to the right, I shot several hundred pictures (with my phone). We tried different things with the balloons: walking, jumping, sitting. . . .

USE WHAT YOU HAVE

Since the beginning of Bag-all, I have used my family as models for the mood images. The simple explanation is that I didn't have any money to pay real models. Luckily for me, my girls and husband don't mind being in pictures (and are pretty cute, if you ask me).

Celeste making jump number 352 . . .

@bag_all
INSTAGRAM

Instagram is one of the best marketing tools available: it is free, easy, and quick to use. You can post images of your new products as well as special offers.

On Bag-all's Instagram account, @bag_all, I post a mix of images from my life in New York and images of Bag-all's products. Personally, I think brands that only post product images get boring. I want to know more about the story of the brand and the people behind it. That's why I share my personal life on Instagram. Bag-all is such an integrated part of my family's life, almost like a fourth child, so to us this makes perfect sense.

Whenever we do something, such as taking a trip to the beach, I take the opportunity to snap pictures of the family with the bags. We use them anyway, so why not?

Celeste walking to the store on Mott Street. There are always photo opportunities . . .

Many pictures on Bag-all's Instagram have nothing to do with bags. They are all about inspiration.

Margaux hitting the beach on Fire Island outside New York.

Caprice on our rooftop in New York City.

Furillen, Gotland. An island in the south of Sweden.

MIXING IT UP

On Bag-all's Instagram, there is a mix of pictures of our products and pictures from my family's life in New York and Sweden as well as from our travels.

Girls with the Christmas Collection.

Caprice in Sweden with a new children's shoe bag.

photo: olssonlinda1975

photo: @cassandreabill

photo: jonnakivilahti

#bagall ♥
POSTS BY
CUSTOMERS

photo: @extrapetite

Lingerie

Pompes

Bijoux

Maquillage

Chaussu

photo: @onodigisnyggt

N°4
MYBAG
NYC

SHOPPING

N°5
MYB

LOVE

photo: @onodigisnyggt

photo: @leahvvar

photo: @annaminh

AMAZEMENT

When I started Bag-all's Instagram, I had not at all expected people to post their own images of the bags. I am blown away by the level of work put into these pictures. We often repost these pictures on @bag_all.

I am sooo grateful for this!!

photo: @yens_

photo: @myohhmy

photo: @hundrafytioellan

photo: @makeri14

PS. This is my sister's super cute store in Stockholm, Makeri 14.

Not-to-do LISTS, & other no's

As you have probably noticed, I am a very big fan of making lists of things to do. In fact, I believe if something is not on a list, it is unlikely that it is ever going to happen. Not only does writing things down help your memory, but the act of putting it on paper or in your phone also makes the tasks take on a life of their own, and things start to materialize.

Another great thing about a to-do list is that you get to cross things *off*. The sense of accomplishment is priceless. Right before your eyes, you can see one thing after another getting scratched off the list. It always makes me feel proud of myself – *today I did all these things.* Had they not been on the list I would have forgotten all the many, many tasks I do each day and wouldn't have given myself credit for them.

Once in a while, I have to stop myself from running around doing all those hundreds of big and small things I do every day – and just do nothing at all.

Besides doing nothing at all, I have a long-term **not-to-do** list that is just as important to me.

Not-to-do
LONG-TERM

1 DON'T THINK ABOUT . . .

. . .or get worked up about things that are out of your control.

2 DO NOT STRESS . . .

. . .about everything having to be perfect around the house.

3 DO NOT HANG OUT . . .

. . .with people who take your energy or make you feel uncomfortable in any way. Or with people you can't count on or trust.

4 DO NOT CHANGE . . .

. . . who you are in order to try to fit in.

5 DO NOT COMPARE . . .

. . . yourself to others. Never ever!

6 DO NOT FOLLOW . . .

. . . people on Instagram or Facebook, even if they are your friends, if they stress you out or make you feel excluded. Or perhaps just because you don't like the pictures they publish. (It is so incredibly common that people feel obliged to follow friends although they get a knot in their stomachs, looking at their pictures.) Not following someone does not mean you don't like them.

8 DO NOT ASSUME THE WORST.

9 DO LISTEN . . .

. . . to people's advice, and DO NOT follow it unless your gut tells you to.

If you can find a path with no obstacles, it probably doesn't lead anywhere.

—Frank A. Clark

Celeste and Margaux on their way to the beach in Montauk.

No PLEASE

One of the people who has inspired me the most is Oprah Winfrey. I have learned more important things from watching Oprah's "Super Soul Sunday" than in all my years in school. One thing Oprah said on a show particularly stuck in my head: *"Saying no to someone else often means saying yes to yourself."*

This was extremely powerful, and I could relate as I have often compromised what I want to do in favor of what other people want me to do. Saying no would make me feel guilty. I somehow felt responsible for friends and family members and thought that if I said no to them I would let them down. It never crossed my mind that I could be letting myself down by saying yes to something I didn't want to do. Hearing Oprah's point really freed me from this way of thinking. Because if you say yes when you *feel* no, you are being dishonest with your feelings, and that benefits no one.

Mastin Kip of dailylove.com added a new dimension to this by pointing out: *"'No' is a complete sentence. It requires no explanation."* Also, for the person who receives the "no," there is an opportunity to grow. If they can't handle it, then obviously they don't have your best interest in mind.

A few years back, I started living by this advice by listening to my inner voice and saying no to people who I felt zapped my energy or in any way made me feel uncomfortable. This was obviously a very big step to take and something that was not at all popular with the people I started saying no to. To them it is, of course, much more convenient to keep things as they were.

Although this can be a very painful and hard process, I think it is important to get rid of distractions and negativity in order to move on with your life. I feel like my life is so much more honest now. Saying no to things or people you are not happy with frees up time for the things that are important to you and makes you happy. I honestly don't know if I would have been able to launch Bag-all if I had continued to allow all the distractions that were going on in my life before I started saying *NO*.

When you start your own business, it is wise to expect to make *sacrifices*. Thinking you can come about change without changing stuff in your life is very unrealistic.

Examples of sacrifices you may have to make when starting your own business:

• **Less security**
Starting your own business means you are taking a huge risk. There simply are no guarantees that it will work out.

• **Less money**
You might have to invest your money in your business rather then going on that trip or buying that purse.

• **Less time for yourself**
I work every day of the week and even a couple of hours on the weekends and holidays. If I don't know what is going on with my business I can't relax anyway. So I check my emails, make lists of what to do, and design stuff. Because it is my business I don't find it tiresome—it is rewarding.

Obstacle PEOPLE

Unfortunately, not everyone in your life is helpful. In fact, all of us have people around who are somehow holding us back. I call these people "obstacle people." These people need to be dealt with whether we like it or not. If we don't, they will slow us down, or worse, prevent us from fulfilling our dreams. This is incredibly challenging especially when it comes to family and old friends.

Obstacle people can be people who make you feel badly about yourself, do not encourage you, outright sabotage things you are trying to do, talk about you behind your back, etc.

I figure there are two ways of dealing with these people. First, after you recognize that they are obstacle people, you can make up your mind to stop *caring*. You will not let what they say or do change your mood or your quest.

The second approach is to use the concept of "teaching people how they should treat you," by forcing them to find a new strategy when dealing with you.

For example, if you let people who are bossy, demanding, or aggressive have their way, you are rewarding them for their behavior, and they'll quickly learn that this behavior works. But if you refuse to give in when people approach you in a negative way, they will have to use another tactic with you to get what they want. Remember—it is never too late to tell people in your life that they need to use a different strategy.

It is easy to complain about how we are being treated by pointing a finger at the other person. But know this: when pointing a finger at someone, there will be three fingers that are pointing right back at you. If people are taking you for granted, and if you are feeling used, misused, or even abused, it is because you have taught them that their strategy works, and that they can get away with it.

So, do a self-check: what am I doing to enable their behavior? Then let them know there are new rules in your relationship. If they don't like it, you basically have no choice but to move on to my next point.

The third way of dealing with obstacle people can be perceived as harsh but is sometimes necessary: cut them out of your life. Some of these people won't let you set new rules in your relationship. They prefer things to be exactly as they have always been, as it is more convenient for them. But I think it more important to follow your own path to happiness and fulfillment as a human being than by pleasing others. We only have one shot at life (as far as we know, at least).

"Sometimes you have to UNFOLLOW *people in real life."*
—Anonymous

This is a no-nonsense approach that I think benefits everyone, and women in particular who have been told they need to be pleasant no matter what since they were babies.

72

I also happen to think that this approach in the long run is good for the person you have cut out of your life. They, too, can move on from an unhealthy relationship and grow as a human being from this experience.

> *"Before you diagnose*
> *yourself with depression*
> *or* LOW SELF-ESTEEM,
> *first make sure you*
> *are not, in fact,*
> *surrounded by* ASSHOLES. *"*
> —Anonymous

There are two other kinds of obstacle people that might appear if you experience success.

COMPARISON PEOPLE

First is a group of people who become jealous. They are not happy about your success and don't want to hear about how you are doing. They are probably comparing themselves to you.

Personally, I have been on both sides of this. When I was younger I would compare myself to people. First, I didn't understand that this was what I was doing, then I didn't know how to stop. Now I know it only makes you miserable. Comparison is a path that leads absolutely nowhere. The quote *"Comparison is the death of joy,"* by Mark Twain, is so true.

When I decided to start focusing on myself instead and what *I* could do to perhaps make this world a

little better, I stopped putting my attention on what other people were doing.

Lately, I have been on the other side of this where some people seem to be bothered by my business doing well. This is quite hard to deal with as I don't want to make them feel bad or inferior in any way. I simply avoid talking about my business with them, and of course, they don't ask.

These days, social media can sometimes feel like an obstacle person, where people go out of their way to show a "perfect" life. It can be really hard to not feel excluded or think that your own life is way more boring and unglamorous. But remember this: you don't have to follow people on social media if it makes you uncomfortable. Not following them does not mean you don't like them. Choose to follow people who inspire you and make you feel good.

Of course, the absolute majority of people are really, truthfully, heartfelt-happy about what is going on with Bag-all. I had never dreamed that people would be so kind and generous with their support! This blows me away and fills me with energy to work harder and try to reach higher!

In Sweden, we have this lovely saying: *"Shared joy is double the joy!"*

FAIR-WEATHER FRIENDS

The second group are the people who were not interested in you before your business was a success. Suddenly, they are extremely interested in you and what you do.

These are your "fair-weather friends," who will be gone the second the going gets tough.

Helpful PEOPLE

At the opposite end of the spectrum are the people who help and empower you. These can be friends or family, a teacher, or even a person you only met once but who happened to say something that helps you along your path. They can also be people you have never met but read about. One of the people who has inspired me the most is, in fact, dead: Eleanor Roosevelt.

She was married to American president Franklin D. Roosevelt and came to be known as one of the most outspoken women in the White House. During her husband's presidency, Eleanor gave press conferences, wrote a newspaper column, and traveled extensively across the US to understand and help poor people in the country. After Franklin's death, she served at the United Nations, focusing on human rights and women's issues. Eleanor was also the queen of quotes. All the following quotes are from her and have meant something to me in one way or another.

"Well-behaved women rarely make history."

I have felt many, many times that people, men and women, perceive me as demanding/annoying/bossy when I want to get things done the way I want them. In a man, these qualities are viewed as a good traits—he "knows what he wants" and "gets things done." But for a woman, it's a different story. We have to fight to get things the way we want them, and along the way we have to take a lot of heat for it.

When I was younger, I felt that it was really hard to push my ideas through, and I typically didn't want to be viewed as unpleasant. These days I know that if I don't do it my way I will regret it later. If people don't like it, I don't care because I am the one who will have to live with the consequences. Honestly, the only times I regret something is when I don't listen to my own intuition and go with what I think other people might like better. Which brings me to the next two quotes:

"Do what you feel in your heart to be right— for you will be criticized anyway."

"A woman is like a tea bag; you never know how strong it is until it's in hot water."

So true! You need to be put through hard times to know your own strength. When those bad things happen to you, you might feel that it is all very unfair. But once you come out on the other side, you are much stronger as you now know you can handle the tough times.

Now—drum roll—another amazing quote:

"No one can make you feel inferior without your consent."

Only if you agree with what a person is saying can it have any value. Absolutely no one, but you, has control over your brain!

You can only be insulted/hurt/put down by a person if you decide that what they have to say has some truth to it. For example, if a person told you that the moon is cheese, you wouldn't actually think the moon is cheese. If you decide that you don't agree with what they are saying, people's words can't hurt you at all. More often than not, what a person (including you) says to other people has everything to do with themselves (yourself) and not the person hearing it. When you realize this, basically no one can insult you ever again!

The next quote might be my favorite quote of all time!

"Great minds discuss ideas. Average minds discuss events. Small minds discuss people."

People are obsessed with talking about other people. But aren't conversations about ideas much greater? They make us feel better and open our minds. Gossiping about others really is only a reflection of ourselves. What this smart woman said is true! Dear Eleanor, when I grow up I want to be exactly like you!!

Another person who just happened to say something to me that helped me along my path was fashionista and business woman Anine Bing.

Anine has built a fashion empire with her husband, Nicolai. I was styling Anine for a fashion shoot and complaining about how much I had to work to get my business going. I felt I was working around the clock and it was never enough. Then Anine said:

"Jennifer, starting your own business is not work, it is a lifestyle."

That was such an "aha" moment for me!

I stopped counting the hours I put into the business and started thinking of my situation as a way of life. Just shifting my own way of thinking from work mode to lifestyle mode meant I no longer felt overwhelmed but accepting and excited about my new life style.

MORE HELPFUL PEOPLE

Helpful people are truly invaluable. If possible, you should try to surround yourself with people who want the best for you, are genuinely happy for you, and encourage you. When you feel like you can be yourself and don't have to change in order to fit in, you know you are around the right people.

I am extremely grateful to have so many people in my life who support me in different ways. No (wo)man is an island.

the greatest of the human freedoms is to choose their own attitude in every given circumstance.

—Bruno Bettelheim, psychologist and expert in fairy tales

STAFF

Finding helpful people on your path can be very hard. But one thing is for sure—you need to find them—because in the long run you cannot do everything yourself. If your business is going to grow, you will need staff to take over certain areas of responsibility. I have discovered that finding good staff is the most challenging part of growing the business. Having good staff is the most amazing thing in the world as they will help you grow and bring great ideas to the table. On the other hand, having bad staff can truly be devastating, especially to a small business.

Female BUSINESS

Much of the business world is male-dominated, and too often women are patted on the head.

I have heard from men: *how cute, you are selling some little bags and playing shop*. The same guys view apps, games, and technology with awe. Most tech companies are heavily leveraged and have not made a single dime. Bag-all, on the other hand, has made money from day one, and I have built it by reinvesting the profits in new inventory. These days, this method is considered very old school.

In the male-dominated business world, you are expected to use your head, not your heart or your intuition. Traditionally, business has been about achieving goals and being highly competitive with a focus on a linear, left-brain way of thinking.

The more feminine way of doing business is multi-tasking, relationship-building, and using the creative right brain. Women are more prone to start on a smaller scale and not immediately go for the corner office with a view. Running a business "the female way" causes some to not take you seriously. However, lately there has been a shift in the perception of these qualities within business. There is an increasing understanding that integrating classic business practices with feminine communication and management methods delivers better results. It also benefits employees, business owners, and, in the end, the customers and society as a whole.

I think that because I was over forty years old when I started my business, I have had the courage to rely heavily on my gut feeling when it comes to making business decisions.

For instance, I sold my bags via one of the largest e-commerce stores the first year. As it turned out, being a vendor was a horrible experience for my growing company. We would get charge-backs (fines) for random things, it was impossible to get ahold of a person to get explanations or dispute charges, the payment terms were extremely bad for the vendor but very beneficial for the e-commerce site and so on and so forth. I found their business methods to be fear-based and "one way." To me, this is not a constructive way of doing business or living life. In the end, I decided to stop doing business with them altogether. I didn't want to have a knot in my stomach, no matter how much money it would bring me.

Of course, doing business is about making a profit in the end, but there is more than one way of defining success. For me, profit is important, but more important is staying true to your values and making sure the business gives back to society and the environment. Women typically understand that if you don't integrate your personal values, your vision, and your sense of purpose within your business, you won't be fulfilled as a human being. If you conduct your business with a mindset of being fair and trying to do fulfilled, not only will you feel good, but your customers will pick up on it and see that your brand is genuine. They become more than customers—they become loyal supporters.

FEMINISM

Many people, even women, are reluctant to call themselves feminists. To me, the only explanation is that they don't fully understand the meaning of the word. To me, being a feminist is a no-brainer.

It is obvious that women and men should have equal rights, possibilities, and salary. In the US, women are only getting 79 percent of the salary men make. In many other cultures, women are routinely being suppressed—they cannot choose what to wear, they are not allowed to work, or they are being mutilated. Something very alarming is that one third* of women worldwide are exposed to physical or sexual violence in their lifetime.

For as long as these things are happening, I believe everyone, women and men alike, need to keep being feminists and understand that there is still a long road ahead.

CHARITY

I am a big believer in paying it forward. Everyone in my family and Bag-all has Kiva accounts where we donate money to entrepreneurs around the world. Kiva works with micro loans to help underprivileged people develop their businesses, allowing them to support themselves and their communities. The entrepreneurs pay the loans back and you can then re-lend the money to another business. If you decide to become a loan-giver, feel free to join team Bag-all. That way we can work together toward prosperity for all. Please check this wonderful organization out at www.kiva.org.

* Statistics from unwomen.org and WHO

there is a special place in hell for women who don't help each other.

—Madeleine Albright
Former United States Secretary of State

MENTORS & WOMEN

Some women I know have been lucky enough to have mentors in their life. I have never had one. Once, I asked an older woman who worked for the same newspaper as I did if she would be my mentor. But no, she wasn't interested.

In my experience, women are unfortunately very bad at helping each other. Oftentimes they seem to be threatened by younger females. I think women have a lot to learn from men in this respect. Men bond, play golf, and promote each other. Women must start doing the same thing and not see other females as competition. We will never have an equal society unless women start being equal among themselves.

The silver lining to this cloud is the following: Because I have had to figure everything out myself—how to produce a product, create a web page, photograph the products, pack and ship, etc., I know my business inside out. Nothing has been outsourced. I have an intimate understanding of the role each person working for Bag-all plays because I have done all of their jobs.

BE careful
WHAT YOU WISH FOR

You MIGHT get it . . .
Bag-all was GROWING quickly and I needed a
space — urgently. I found my DREAM space, but it
slipped through my fingers . . .
Luckily!

I started Bag-all out of our house. This was not a problem as it had been part of the original plan. Remember, I had even put on my list that the product needed to be flat and easy to store so I could work from home.

I really recommend starting your business from your house if it is possible. It saves you a lot of money and makes your family a part of the business. It's really helpful if your family understands what you do, and it is, of course, an added bonus if they can help you out. I have had both family and friends helping me out with the bags. Like the time we had to change the ribbons from purple to black on a thousand bags. Or when I forgot to tell the factory to iron the bags and had to iron four thousand bags myself.

space
NEEDED
urgently

After our first gift show, I realized I had to place larger orders from the factory since we sold out of many prints during the show. With the larger orders coming in and going out, my daughter Margaux had to give up her room so we could store the boxes.

Soon that space was not big enough either. We had boxes all over our apartment, in the living room, in the master bedroom, under and on top of the dining table. For six months, we couldn't sit at our dinner table to eat.

I started to realize that the box situation in our house couldn't go on any longer. The boxes were driving my

Above is Margaux's room before I started Bag-all. On the left is what it looked like after I had to start placing larger orders. We were quickly running out of space at home.

family and me insane. We urgently needed to find Bag-all an office space. However, while looking at office spaces in New York City, I could not believe how expensive they were.

This gave me the idea of a combined office/store space. Customers had been emailing, asking where they could see the entire collection. So a store seemed like a great solution. This way, perhaps the sales in the store could even cover part of the rent. The more I thought about it, the more I got a vision of a Bag-all store in one of the old store spaces in Nolita.

Nolita means "NOrth of Little ITAly." It is a cool little area east of the famous Soho shopping district in New York. In this area, smaller brands have boutiques with really cool and unique things. Many of the store spaces have beautiful original bay windows in carved wood. That was exactly what I wanted. I especially zoomed in

Our living room slowly getting absorbed by boxes.

> *"The elevator to SUCCESS is out of order. You will have to use the STAIRS . . . One step at a time."*
>
> —Joe Girard

Orders coming in. Dealing with it all on our living room floor.

on an area of only six square blocks. The broker wanted me to look in other areas, but my heart was set on Nolita. I think that the more specific you can be with what you want, the more likely it is you will get it.

I walked around Nolita to get a better idea of what would be the ideal location for Bag-all. All of a sudden, there it was—the perfect space on Spring Street! It had the old bay window with original wood carvings. It had a sign on the window saying FOR RENT. I called the number and met up with the broker a day later. I was totally in love with this space. It looked exactly like what I had envisioned—and it was in my budget. The only drawback was that it was very small and had no storage space.

But I was blinded by love and didn't mind those "minor" issues at all. I thought that somehow we could make it work, my space and I.

The broker worked out all the details with the owner, who approved Bag-all as a tenant. We agreed on the rent, the move-in date, and the rest of the details. All that was left was to sign the lease. So I waited for the lease to come, and I waited, and then waited some more. I called the broker who assured me that it would come any day . . .

Finally, a couple of weeks later the broker called me to let me know that the landlord had decided to give the space to another tenant. I was devastated. Our love affair was over before it even began.

21

First day at Mott Street. So much work and fun lay ahead.

84

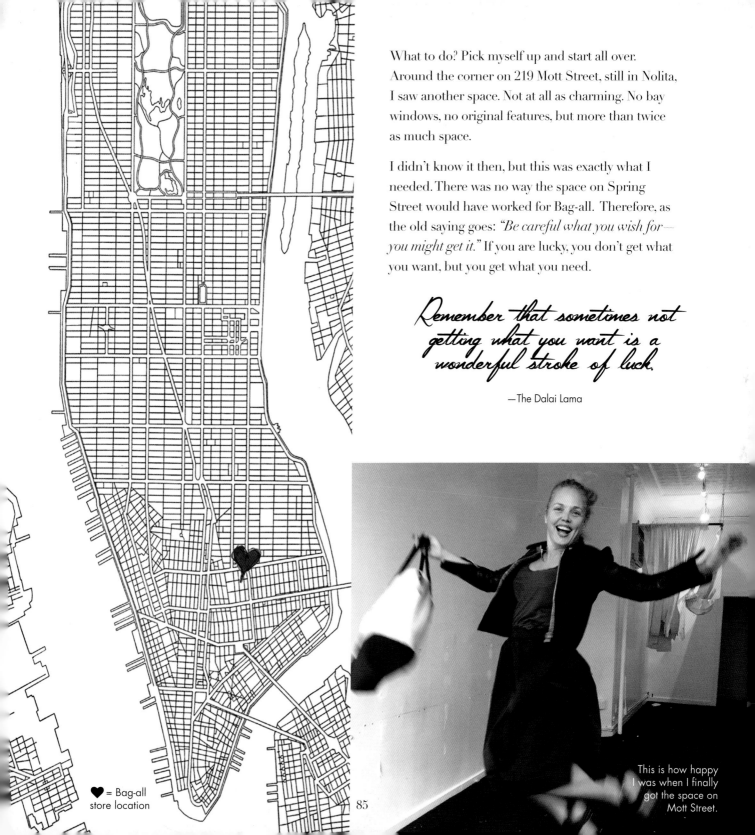

What to do? Pick myself up and start all over. Around the corner on 219 Mott Street, still in Nolita, I saw another space. Not at all as charming. No bay windows, no original features, but more than twice as much space.

I didn't know it then, but this was exactly what I needed. There was no way the space on Spring Street would have worked for Bag-all. Therefore, as the old saying goes: *"Be careful what you wish for— you might get it."* If you are lucky, you don't get what you want, but you get what you need.

Remember that sometimes not getting what you want is a wonderful stroke of luck.

—The Dalai Lama

♥ = Bag-all store location

85

This is how happy I was when I finally got the space on Mott Street.

MAKING
mood
boards
helps you FOCUS
and SEE *your ideas.*

W hen I worked as a stylist I always used to create mood boards for my fashion stories. I would search the web for great inspirational photos, then compile them in a document. That way I would get an actual image of my vision. I learned that this was a great way not only for me to focus, but also for everyone else involved in the photo shoot to get on the same page.

Making a mood board works the same way as writing a list. The creation of the boards is the first step to bringing ideas to life. Therefore, it is a great thing to do for your life goals as well. If you collect images of all the things you want in your life, it gives you an understanding of where you want to go, and you can start on your path.

Images are not hard to find; they are everywhere on the Internet or in magazines. Print them out, cut them out, or take them yourself and create a mood board in your phone. . . .

Below is the mood board I made for Mott Street. I wanted the store to feel genuine to the Nolita area in New York. I Googled old pictures of Mott Street back in the 1800s when the buildings were built to get an idea of what the stores might have looked like. I photographed an original mosaic floor (top left) in another store in the area and then bought similar tiles. As for the furniture— it is all vintage, of course.

Bag-all store
Mott Street
New York

before
RENOVATIONS

Hubby all dusty after tearing the walls down.

Exposing the bricks.

Basement at Mott Street before . . .

. . .we decided to paint the floors yellow.

219 MOTT STREET

People who come to the Bag-all store on Mott Street think that everything in the space is original. However, when I got the space it had interiors from the sixties with black wall-to-wall carpet. When we decorated the store, we added original-looking details.

progress . . .

Opening the store has been one of the best moves I have ever made. It is a fantastic feeling being able to connect with the customers. People are very generous with praise for the Bag-all concept, and they come with great suggestions. Many of our prints are made because people have asked for those particular bags. Moreover, we can test new ideas in the store by putting samples on the sales floor, and that way we hear if customers like them.

First customers. A group of ladies from Gothenburg, Sweden.

...finished!

When we got Mott Street,
it was only Micke and me
who could jump for joy.
Now we are six!

the brooklyn
PRINT SHOP

When we first moved into Mott street, the store felt as large as a palace. I thought that it was large enough to last us for years. However, after only six months the storage space was overcrowded with boxes and the staff could not fit in the little office. Yet again, the business had outgrown its space. I clearly had to start looking for another space for Bag-all.

Simultaneously, another thing was happening; we were getting many requests for custom orders, meaning people and companies wanted to buy our bags with their own print or logo. Having these orders done in China was not only time consuming but also required shipping from across the world, which is something I don't want for Bag-all. So I started to dream about opening my own screen print shop/studio in New York. The more I thought about it, the more I realized there were many advantages to the idea:

• Locally printed bags would minimize transportation.
• Custom orders could be produced quickly.
• We would never sell out of a print again. If a print sold out, we could simply print more of it ourselves.
• It would give us the ability to create a new product in no time. As opposed to waiting for samples from China for weeks, we could make a new print in thirty minutes.
• Storage space. We needed to rescue the Mott Street store from drowning in boxes.
• Perhaps it could even be large enough to house a small studio to photograph the products.

As usual, I started by creating a mood board with images and words of what I wanted the space to look like and added all the things I had on my wish list:

• Industrial type of space, with high ceilings and large windows.
• Large enough to hold screen printing equipment and function as a warehouse.
• A studio area where the staff and I could be inspired to work creatively.

At my desk in the new office in Brooklyn.

The studio space the first day.

93

The space in BROOKLYN *is a new, exciting*
phase in the Bag-all STORY. *My absolute favorite thing is to be*
CREATIVE *and get things done – at once!*

BAG DU JOUR
Print of the day are the High heel Sandals. They had been sold out for a while. But not any more!

When I thought about a dream space for the printing studio, I remembered a run-down but very cool building in Brooklyn where I had once bought a shelf for the store. Again, my broker tried to talk me into looking in other areas, but I felt strongly that this place would be a good fit for us. Luckily, there was a space just the right size that was empty.

Creating a printing studio was another big step and investment for Bag-all. The screen printing would add another business leg to stand on, which of course was good. On the other hand, it would mean more things to take care of. However, weighing the pros and cons, I concluded that we should go for it. Today, I am so happy we did this as we now have the freedom to be incredibly creative and try new ideas whenever we want to.

GROWING PAIN & GAIN

Having a business is both fun and challenging. There will always be more things that need to be done and new ways to grow. Bag-all is still in a start-up phase, but is growing very quickly.

At this point, Bag-all is selling bags to stores in over twenty-five countries and in thirty-five of the US states. All money earned goes straight back into the business. Sometimes this can be frustrating as you see the growth on paper but not in your wallet, which looks about the same as when I started. Constantly having to buy more inventory and make other big investments is one of the most challenging things about growing when you are self-financed. On the other hand, the freedom of fully owning your own business is worth it to me. I can do things only because I think it is fun or important. Every decision I make does not have to make a profit. I can decide to support a local artisan group by buying their product rather then a cheaper item that would make more money. For instance I bought beautiful pom poms from a Thai mountain tribe. They were so expensive we made almost no money on them. However, the tribe used the money to send their children to school in the village. This was all the profit I needed.

The display in PLAZASTYLE's Ginza store in Tokyo.

TOKYO CALLING

The Japanese department store PLAZASTYLE did amazing pop-up stores in several locations during 2016. They had gone above and beyond to recreate the feel of the Bag-all store in New York City. They even recreated the floor tiles and the subway tiles from the walls at Mott Street.

A spring day in Central
Park by the Boathouse.

98

praise
& GRATITUDE

You, more than anyone else, are WORTH
your PRAISE *. Go on — tell yourself*
how GREAT *you are!*

A few years ago, someone told me that the brain cannot distinguish between inner and outer praise. This means that when you tell yourself, *"I did really well today,"* your brain reacts, chemically, in the same exact way as if someone else praised you. Praise releases endorphins and makes you feel really good. The same goes for criticism. It is easy to think, *"Ugh, I look fat in these jeans,"* or *"I'm not doing as well as this or that person."* Every time you have a negative thought about yourself, your brain reacts in the same way as if someone else had insulted you. So be careful about what you tell yourself.

If you are aware of this, which most people are not, you can easily boost your self-esteem. That's right, you don't need anyone else's approval — convenient, right? All you need to do when those negative thoughts are creeping up is to turn them on their head. *"I look great in these jeans. Big booties are all the rage!"* or *"That person is doing great — good for them. I'll soon be there myself. Now how can I get there?"*

Another thing that works like a charm is feeling gratitude. The more grateful you are, the more blessings you will receive. It works!

"GRATITUDE opens the door to . . . the power, the wisdom, the creativity of the UNIVERSE. You open the door through gratitude."

—Deepak Chopra

Many years ago I was introduced to the idea of a Gratitude Journal by Oprah. She spoke about the importance of being grateful on her show and she mentioned that she kept a gratitude journal. It can be a notebook where you record some of the things you are grateful for each day. What you write down can be anything, even small things, like a stranger holding the door for you, someone's smile on the bus, or simply appreciating the existence of a flower. It can also be bigger things like a new job, a new trip planned, or your family. So, a few years ago I started my own gratitude journal, using an app on my phone. It was surprisingly easy to come up with the things I was grateful for. The more I focused on these things, the more often they seemed to appear in my life.

If you make gratitude a habit, you can train yourself to feel grateful throughout each day by acknowledging all the small moments of grace.

"I know for SURE that what we dwell on is who we BECOME."

—Oprah Winfrey

In addition to the gratitude journal, it is a great idea to create a "I did good" journal. Why not keep a record of the things you accomplish every day? Again, it can be the tiniest things. For some people, it can be *"I got out of bed," "I made that phone call I had postponed — yes!"* You soon start to realize how much you actually get done every single day.

When I do good, I feel good. When I do bad, I feel bad. that's my religion

—Abraham Lincoln, President of the United States

Then why not give yourself some credit for it? Tell yourself, *"Good job, buddy!"*

It is also very important to remember to give praise to others. When I was a child, I remember how my grandmother used to say: *"Jennifer, you did something really good and now I am going to give you praise for it."* I recall how silly I thought it was to announce praise. But today I know that she was truly on to something: the importance of praise. By pointing it out to me, her praise did not pass unnoticed. See, I still remember it today. Praise makes us feel good about ourselves, helps build up our self-esteem, and makes us want to reach higher heights.

Good thing it's not a problem if we don't have other people around to point out how great we are, because we can just *praise ourselves*.

101

Trying to
live
LIKE WE
learn

No one is PERFECT.
*But every day we can all make
small,* BETTER *choices
for the environment.*

In our summer-house in Sweden, we barely have anything new. In the kitchen, we have my grandmother's old kitchen sofa. We found the stepping stool at a flea market, and the chairs were left in the house by the previous owners. The table is vintage IKEA. Actually, some of IKEA's furniture is being sold at auctions these days.

Photo: Jenny Brandt

No one is perfect, and it's impossible to do everything right all the time. Sometimes you just have to be practical. But the more small choices we make every day trying to think in a sustainable manner, the better. At Bag-all, we try to think in a "reuse" way (see pages 110–111).

At home, we also do our best to be environmentally friendly. As I already mentioned, most of our furniture is vintage. We don't own a dryer for our clothes. Instead we let everything air dry. We don't own a car in New York, and we mostly use public transportation (with the added bonus that it is much cheaper and that we never have to think about parking). What's more, we recycle everything that can be recycled.

It is easy to think: "It doesn't matter if I change my behavior since so many others are not changing theirs." This is NOT true. What every single one of us does, *does* matter, big time. With small steps, we can all make big changes for a better future for our shared planet.

20 small things YOU can do

*Examples from: www.50waystohelp.com

1 RECYCLE GLASS

Recycled glass reduces related air pollution by 20 percent and related water pollution by 50 percent. If it isn't recycled it can take a million years to decompose. Every ton of glass recycled saves the equivalent of nine gallons of fuel oil needed to make glass from virgin materials.

The bathroom counter is a repurposed antique cabinet from India.

2 RETHINK BOTTLED WATER

Nearly 90 percent of plastic water bottles are not recycled, instead taking thousands of years to decompose. Buy a reusable container and fill it with tap water, a great choice for the environment, your wallet, and possibly your health, as tap water is highly controlled.

3 WRAP CREATIVELY

You can reuse gift bags, bows, and wrapping paper, but you can also make something unique by using old maps, cloths, or even newspaper. Flip a paper bag inside out and give your child stamps or markers to create their own wrapping paper that's environmentally friendly and extra special for the recipient.

4 CHANGE YOUR LIGHT

If every household in the United States replaced one regular lightbulb with one of those new compact fluorescent bulbs, the pollution reduction would be equivalent to removing one million cars from the roads.

5 GO VEGETARIAN ONCE A WEEK

One less meat-based meal a week helps the planet and your diet. For example: It requires 2,500 gallons of water to produce one pound of beef. By reducing your meat intake you will also save some trees. For each hamburger that originated from animals raised on rainforest land, approximately 55 square feet of the forest have been destroyed.

6 INVEST IN YOUR OWN COFFEE CUP

Invest in a reusable cup, which not only cuts down on waste, but also keeps your beverage hot longer. Most coffee shops will happily fill your own cup, and many even offer you a discount in exchange!

7 BUY LOCAL FOOD

Consider the amount of pollution created to get your food from the farm to your table. When possible, buy from local farmers or farmers' markets, which supports your local economy and reduces the amount of greenhouse gas created when products are flown or trucked in. And never EVER buy water from another continent than where you currently are.

Celeste in a chair that I inherited from my grandmother. The table and painting are flea market finds.

"Your life does not get better by CHANCE. *It gets better by* CHANGE. *"*
—Jim Rohn

105

8 SKIP THE STRAW

Each year in the US 138 billion straws are thrown away. This is totally unnecessary garbage— we do not *need* straws to drink.

9 USE ONE LESS PAPER NAPKIN

During an average year, an American uses approximately 2,200 napkins—around six each day. If everyone in the US used one less napkin a day, more than a billion pounds of napkins could be saved from landfills each year.

10 CHOOSE MATCHES

Most lighters are made out of plastic and filled with butane fuel, both petroleum products. Since most lighters are considered "disposable," over 1.5 billion end up in landfills each year. When choosing matches, pick cardboard over wood. Wood matches come from trees, whereas most cardboard matches are made from recycled paper.

11 HANG DRY

Get a clothesline to air dry your clothes. Saves you money AND clothes last longer.

12 RECYCLE

Twenty recycled aluminium cans can be made with the energy it takes to manufacture one brand new one. There are 63 million newspapers printed each day in the US. Of these, 44 million, or about 69 percent of them, will be thrown away. Recycling just the Sunday papers would save more than half a million trees every week.

13 TAKE SHORTER SHOWERS

Every two minutes you save on your shower can conserve more than ten gallons of water. If everyone in the US saved just one gallon from their daily shower, over the course of a year it would equal twice the amount of freshwater withdrawn from the Great Lakes every day.

NO PAPER STATEMENTS

Ask your bank and other places you get paper bills and statements from to stop sending those and replace them with e-bills. If all households in the US paid their bills online and received electronic statements instead of paper, some estimates show that we'd save 18.5 million trees every year. *14*

All photos: Jenny Brandt

15 RECYCLE CELL PHONES

The average cell phone lasts around eighteen months, which means 130 million phones will be retired each year. If they go into landfills, the phones and their batteries introduce toxic substances into our environment. There are plenty of reputable programs where you can recycle your phone, many that benefit noble causes.

16 PICNIC WITH A CONSCIENCE

Never use disposable paper or plastic plates. You can either buy plastic plates that can be reused hundreds of times or use other plastic containers you have around the house to eat from. The same goes for plastic knives, forks, and spoons. Just bring your regular cutlery to the picnic.

17 USE BOTH SIDES OF THE PAPER

American businesses throw away 21 million tons of paper every year, equal to 175 pounds per office worker. For a quick and easy way to halve this, set your printer's default option to print double-sided (duplex printing). And when you're finished with your documents, don't forget to take them to the recycling bin.

18 PLASTIC NOT SO FANTASTIC

Each year there are 500 billion plastic bags used worldwide. They are not biodegradable, and are making their way into our oceans, and subsequently, the food chain. Stronger, reusable bags such as tote bags are an inexpensive and readily available option.

19 DIAPER WITH A CONSCIENCE

By the time a child is toilet trained, a parent will change between five thousand and eight thousand diapers, adding up to approximately 3.5 million tons of waste in US landfills each year. Whether you choose cloth or a more environmentally friendly disposable, you're making a choice that has a much gentler impact on our planet.

20 SECOND HAND

Consider buying items from a second-hand store. Toys, bicycles, rollerblades, and other age- and size-specific items are quickly outgrown. Second-hand stores often sell these items in excellent condition since they are used for such a short period of time, and will generally buy them back when you no longer need them.

We use old potato crates to store our pots and pans. The cabinets above the counter were there when we bought the house. The previous owner told us they had built the cabinets out of old office furniture. I love the sunny yellow color inside.

The subway is by far our favorite mode of transportation. Even when we deliver bags, we will take the subway.

PLEASE *reuse*

waste

Here, Micke and I are on our way to deliver one of the first orders we got in New York. You can imagine that the client was surprised to see the owner showing up hand delivering the goods.

In the history of Bag-all, we have only had to buy two cardboard boxes. All other shipments have been made in boxes we found on the streets of New York. In New York, we put the garbage and our recyclables out on the curb two days a week. In our neighborhood there are many big stores that receive their goods in hundreds of boxes a week. They are clean, and neatly tied together in

Micke found a gold mine!

bundles. Just waiting for us to come pick them up.

We basically recycle before the recycle. My estimate is that we save several thousand dollars each year on this, and most important, we save the environment from having to make and dispose of all those boxes.

REDUCE

From
Bag-all
with
♥

www.bag-all.com
131 West 77 Street #4
New York, NY 10024

BIODEGRADABLE
♻

We pack in recycled materials

Please Reuse
Waste Reduce

Bag-all
219 Mott Street
New York, NY 10012
www.bag-all.com

Our shopping bags are made from recycled paper and we use a stamp to put our logo on them.

One hard nut to crack was how to ship the bags. I tried all sorts of envelopes and finally found a biodegradable mailer bag made from recycled material. This bag will, should it end up in nature, decompose.

At Bag-all, we reuse all materials.

The bags come in poly bags from the factory. We reuse these when sending out items to customers. A reused plastic bag is of course not as crisp as a new one so we have created a sticker (see above) to put on the packs so our customers can understand why the poly bags looks used.

Margaux in a dress
she created herself
from an old curtain.

CREATING
creativity
No point in sitting there WAITING *for* CREATIVITY *to happen. You have to* WORK *for it—just like everything else in life.*

Creativity is an important part of life, in my opinion. Once in a while people tell me, *"You are so creative and I could never do that."* I don't think that this is true at all. You have to work to get good at being creative just like anything else.

Every child I have ever met likes to draw and does it even though they don't know "how" to. They don't ask themselves: "Do I *know* how to draw?" No, they go ahead and do it. I think that schools actually have a big part in killing this creativity when the kids get a bit older and teachers start grading their work. All of a sudden children can get the idea that they don't know how to draw or perhaps see that

Cappi in front of a Picasso in the Guggenheim museum in NYC.

to live a creative life we must lose our fear of being wrong.

—Joseph Chilton Pearce

another child is considered better at drawing then they are. Therefore they conclude that they should stop. This is truly sad and wrong. No one is to say what is good or bad when it comes to creativity. All sorts of expression is equally good.

Another misconception about creativity is that it is something that just "comes over you" like some sort of divine inspiration. The idea is that all of a sudden you start channelling a higher power. I think that in rare cases, things like that can happen, but in most cases it is a question of getting started. You don't really need to have an idea when you start; just sit down and put something, anything, on paper. Then add something else and then the next thing. Eventually you will have created something. When done, do not judge yourself and do not compare your creation with what other people have created.

At the Whitney Museum in New York. The girls are listening to a childrens version of a guided tour in their headphones.

114

painting pottery.

Creative ADVICE

Margaux loves fashion. Ever since I can remember she has been interested in what she wears. One summer she found our old curtains and started making a dress out of the fabric. She had a mannequin that was just her size and she started pinning and sewing the dress together. It became the most magnificent dress (you can see it on the previous spread). She was able to make these creations because she had the tools available to her.

• Make sure you (and your kids) **have the tools** to be creative. I always make sure to have lots of pens and paper in the house—at the children's height—so they can access it any time they choose to.

• Don't be afraid to **try your ideas**. No matter how small or insignificant they seem. A small idea can turn out to something much bigger. See Happy Clogs on page 122.

• Get inspired! Go to **museums** (if you live in a place where museums are not available, then go to the web; every significant piece of art ever created is there for free), look at nature, look at buildings, read books, see movies. There is such a wealth of things out there to take part of. Small bits and pieces of other people's work can be part of your work to create something entirely new.

• **Go make things!** In most cities there are public art spaces and museums that have open studios, for instance a craft shop where you can paint pottery.

You can be creative with anything in your life. It doesn't have to be art. It can be cooking, making a cake with all sorts of crazy ingredients . . . or picking a bouquet of flowers that normally wouldn't go together.

Creating fun memories is another way of being creative. One summer, Margaux wanted to host an elegant tea party. She drew beautiful invitations and delivered them to each person in the family. We, of course, were all in and got dressed in fancy clothes. We enjoyed the tea party with the girls' most elegant china (bought at a flea market for $10).

So much fun, so easy to do, almost free and still a very cherished memory.

All dressed up with some place to go . . .

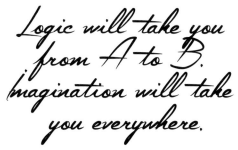

Logic will take you from A to B. Imagination will take you everywhere.

—Albert Einsten

Me ready to attend a fancy tea party.

Caprice in front of a fence made out of old skiis. How genius?!

the purpose of REPURPOSE

shelf unit ...

...to kitchen counter!

When you repurpose something, you take an existing item and give it a new use. Repurposing is a great and fun way of recycling.

You can do it with anything from old furniture to clothes. There are so many inspiring pictures on the Internet: people make sofas out of old tubs and chairs out of an old suitcases ... The possibilities are endless. I have repurposed many times myself, both furniture and clothes. For instance, our old shelf unit became our kitchen counter.

One of the easiest things to repurpose is your own old clothes. For example you can cut a new neckline on an old T-shirt or add beads or stitches to it to give it a new look. You can also quite easily create children's clothes out of your old garments. On the next page you can see examples of clothes I made for the girls when they were smaller.

Besides clothes, you can create fun toys for the kids out of almost anything. Some feathers I found at a flea market made a great headpiece for the children to play with. Repurposing is truly unlimited. Let your imagination take you places!

Celeste with cousin Linus in the headpiece I made out of old feathers.

119

Re-creation NATION

You can repurpose anything. Most likely your house is full of items that could be given a whole new life. An old T-shirt quickly became a new kids' dress.

Baby T-shirts and onesies make great starting points for new creations. I added tulle to Margaux's T-shirt to make it into a super cute dress. In order to get an "old" look I dyed it in regular black tea. It is done by making a strong pot of tea and letting the garment soak in it for approximately thirty minutes.

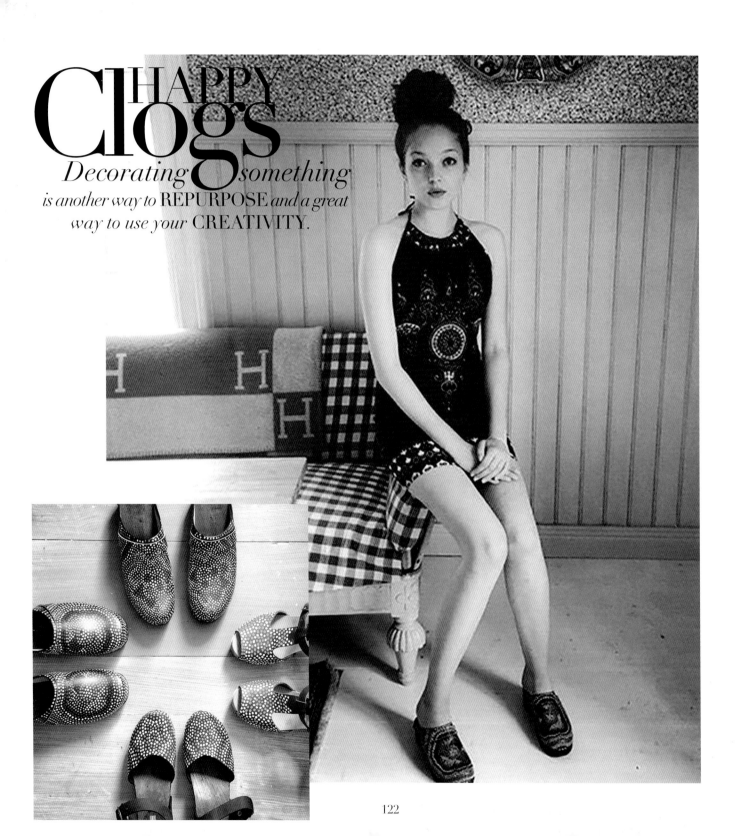

HAPPY Clogs

Decorating something is another way to REPURPOSE *and a great way to use your* CREATIVITY.

Every year we go to Sweden over the summer. And every year the girls have grown out of last year's clogs. Wearing painted clogs is a lovely old Swedish tradition. We, of course, like to paint them ourselves. One summer, I got the idea that I would paint the clogs with dots of color. I was inspired by African bead-work and made a pair for myself. I put an image of the clogs on my Instagram and people started asking if they could buy a pair.

This is where Antonia, left, Souki , my niece, and I painted the clogs.

my "Maasai" clogs.

When I create something I often use pictures for inspiration. For this clog collection I used images of African Maasai bead work. I love the colors and the shapes they make, and using a picture makes it easier to create something new.

My sister, Antonia, thought it would be a great idea if we could start a shoe brand, Happy Clogs, with these painted clogs. And being the optimist that I am, I said, "Sure!" However, we had no idea how popular they would become and we sold so many pairs that the rest of that summer was spent painting clogs.

Redecorating things is a wonderful way to bring old items into a new era and give them your personal touch.

Make visible what, without you, might perhaps never have been seen.

—Joseph Chilton Pearce

123

The WAY WE play

"Jennifer waves
from an OPEN window on the top floor,
and we enter a house that most likely
both PIPPI LONGSTOCKING
and ANNA WINTOUR *would call*
a dream house."

This is an excerpt from an interview I did for the website www.thewayweplay.se. The talented women behind this website are LOUISE RIZELL, KAROLINA BORG, and photographer LINDA ALFVEGREN, lindaa.se. One late summer day, this trio came to visit us at our summerhouse in Sörmland to do a piece for their site. On the following pages is the interview and the dreamy pictures by Linda.

Me and the girls in my summer bedroom.

On the ladder to the treehouse in "Albus."

#selfie

Where: *At the magical summerhouse Ekbacken in Sörmland, two right turns from Stockholm but several miles from reality. Mostly because visiting Ekbacken is like stepping right into a fairytale.*
When: *A late summer day in August 2014 when the warm weather was still lingering and the grass was blowing in the wind.*
How: *Among heavenly dresses, bubbly baths, tree houses, and sparkling games.*

Two right turns from Stockholm and getting closer to Ekbacken, the summer residence of the Jansch family, in Sörmland. We turn onto the small gravel road and anticipate with all our senses that we are getting closer to the idyll.

At the end of the road there is a red wooden house with a gigantic fairy tale–like oak tree, which we later find out has been named Albus by the three sisters, Celeste, 13, Margaux, 9, and Caprice, aka Cappi, 6. Jennifer waves from an open window on the top floor, and we enter a house that most likely both Pippi Longstocking and Anna Wintour would call a dream house.

Jennifer Jansch is the uber-inspiring stylist who was one of the founders of the magazines Mama *and* Family Living. *In 2011 she took the big leap and made her dreams come true by moving to New York with her husband, Micke, and the girls. Jennifer now runs her own business, Bag-all — a brand with a unique eco-friendly idea of reducing garbage by reusing fabric gift bags and storage bags.*

Thank you to the Jansch family for having us over! Your universe moved ours to a slightly more magical dimension.

Tell us about your journey with Bag-all.
Well, I got tired of all the garbage created by gift wrapping around the holiday season each year. By chance I stumbled upon the idea of using reusable gift bags rather then gift wrapping paper. I made some bags for my family and my friends. When I gave the bags to my friends they started using them for other things such as putting their hair dryer in it. That's how the idea for the Organizing Collection was born.

Your best advice as a mother?
Not to say "no" too often to small things when the kids are little. If you do, they won't listen when it's really important. When they get older I don't think a parent should let them "decide" too many things, as that is putting the adult's responsibility on the shoulders of the child. You aren't doing the kids, or yourself, any favor by letting them "rule." Quite the opposite.

But the most important thing is to give them love in overdoses! Kisses and hugs and praise, telling them how much you love them every day. The combination of lots of love and being quite strict is a good one.

What is the hardest thing as a mom?
The hardest thing is making time for myself. I get a really bad conscience whenever I do something for myself rather then spend all my time with them. But as my husband says, "You have to take care of your children's mother." Meaning I have to take care of myself in order to have the energy for them.
Second thing is keeping the house in order. Three kids mess it up in no time, and if you are messy, like I am, it makes matters worse!

*"But the most important thing is to give them love in overdoses!
Kisses and hugs and praise, telling them how much you love them every day.
The combination of lots of love and being quite strict is a good one."*

Caprice in the lower bunk bed. I had these beds made by a local carpenter. They are queen size so two people can sleep in each bed.

What are some of your favorite things in life?

When I see my children's personalities, they are so completely different. To hear their thoughts about different things. I often get "aha" moments from my kids. I also really love being creative. Whenever I put effort into creating something, a great photo, a painting, or sewing something, it makes me feel really good about myself.

What inspires you?

People's energy! I get so much wonderful response from people. They email me, comment on my blog, come up to me in the street . . . Honestly, I had no idea people in general are so generous.

If you had more time?

Work out more, do more yoga, take massages more often.

What makes you happy?

People who care about the environment. Spending time with my family and friends.

What do you do on a Saturday?

Most often I have made tons of plans, which the children can find kind of annoying. I want to take the opportunity to go somewhere, to see new things. If the girls get to decide, they want to be in their pajamas all day.

What does your everyday life look like?

The children, my husband, work, friends, workout/ yoga. Pretty much in that order—during summertime. Wintertime, work comes first.

I get up really early and work a couple of hours while the rest of family is getting out of bed. Then get the kids off to school. Then I work all day until it is time to pick up the girls from school. I hang out with them a couple of hours; we do homework and other activities. Micke most often makes dinner. He's a great chef. After dinner I work a few more hours.

Favorite place?

Ekbacken, our summerhouse in Sweden, and our rooftop terrace in New York. We are so blessed to have these wonderful spots to be in.

What are your dreams at the moment?

A Bag-all store in New York and more people to help me with my business. *

Best vacation spot?

Sörmland, Sweden. And skiing!

How do you decorate the girls' rooms?

Exactly the way they want it.

Food tips?

Put out cucumber, carrot sticks, mini tomatoes on the table before dinner. I have never seen a child who does not eat his/her vegetables then!

Five New York tips?

- *Good shoes to walk everywhere.*
- *Explore Harlem.*
- *Queens is cool, like Brooklyn used to be.*
- *Go to one of the mile-long beaches outside New York on Long Island. Kismet on Fire Island is our favourite.*
- *Eat at Republic on Union Square (and do order the Litchi Martini).*

Text: Karolina Borg www.thewayweplay.se

* This happened a few months after this interview was made.

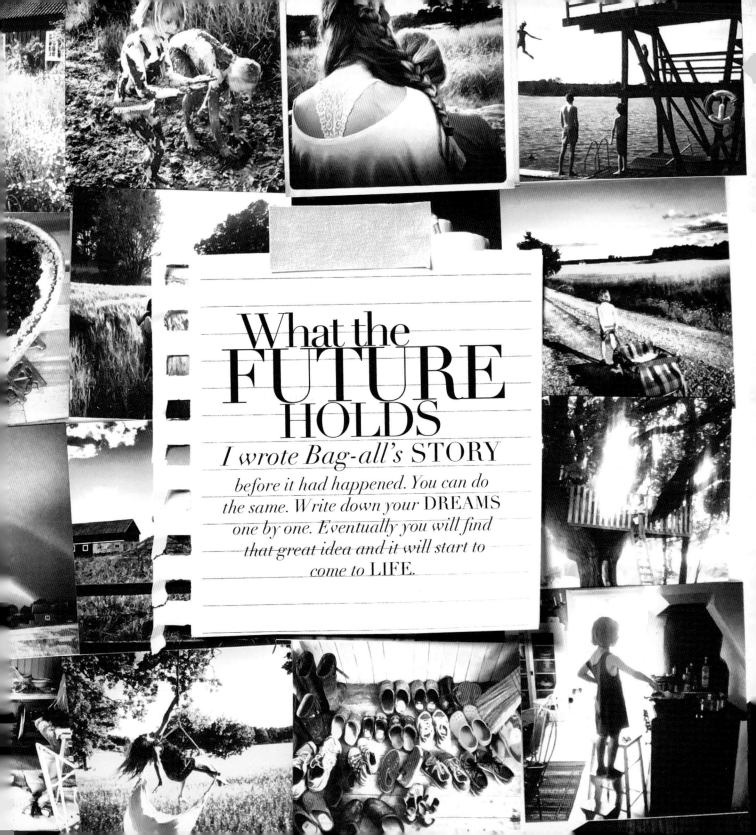

What the FUTURE HOLDS

I wrote Bag-all's STORY

before it had happened. You can do
the same. Write down your DREAMS
one by one. Eventually you will find
that great idea and it will start to
come to LIFE.

A stone I found,
among millions.

We make a living
by what we get,
we make a life
by what we give.

—Winston Churchill

GIVING
thanks

When I do photo shoots, my husband Micke is there to give a helping hand.

HELP & SUPPORT

I am extremely lucky to have a helpful and supportive husband. Micke and I have been married for nineteen years, and we have always worked as a team. He is the yin to my yang. More brave than I am and always encouraging me to take bigger steps than I would have done on my own. He tirelessly helps me in every way that he can and, most important, cheers me on and picks me up when I am down. Without him I don't know if I would have had the courage to let Bag-all grow so quickly. I would have taken smaller steps and not dared those giant leaps.

I also want to give thanks to my daughters, Celeste, Margaux, and Caprice, who are continually there to help out. They have given up their rooms for boxes, helped pack and ship bags, and posed as models in rain and shine without ever complaining.

My mother, Gunilla Wesslau Curman, has been a great support through my life, and she will hop on a plane to New York whenever needed to help out with the girls so I can focus on work. Always being positive and supportive. Her amazing life partner, Robert af Jochnick, has offered advice and all kinds of support above and beyond.

I also want to give a special thanks to Julia Arhammar who has helped me with this book when I have gotten stuck, and Annaminh Braun, my great friend and art director of this book, for being there and putting up with all my changes. There are many, many more people who have been there for me and helped me along my path. I am so grateful for each and every one of you. You know who you are!

Visit our website at www.skyhorsepublishing.com.

10 9 8 7 6 5 4 3 2 1

Library of Congress Cataloging-in-Publication Data is available on file.

Cover design by Annaminh Braun
Cover photo credit by Linda Alfvegren

Print ISBN: 978-1-5107-1878-4
Ebook ISBN: 978-1-5107-1879-1

Printed in China